PRAISE FOR PRO
OTHER PEOPLE'S CHILDREN

"This book is an outstanding resource for organizations that want to create a culture of safety and fulfill their mission of serving our most vulnerable children."

—Juanita Stedman, former juvenile court judge & CEO of Together Georgia

"In their book *Protecting Other People's Children*, Debbie Ausburn and Tom Rawlings provide an important contribution to the field of family and children services. What elevates their work to the 'must-read' pinnacle, though, is that in offering this work, they do so reflecting a clear understanding of the inseparable and critical relationship between an organization's policies, procedures, and processes and an organization's culture."

—Hal Jones, Healthcare Quality Improvement Expert & former CEO of Wellroot Family Services

"A practical guide to safeguarding youth. *Protecting Other People's Children* provides clear, step-by-step instructions for creating effective child protection policies."

—Tim Keller, Center for the Rights of Abused Children

"This book is engaging, informative and a must-read for leaders who manage organizations that work with youth. My compliments to the authors and I highly recommend this book for those who lead in this area serving youth, our future leaders of tomorrow."

—Henry Jackson, President of Buckner Children and Family Services, Inc.

Protecting
Other People's
Children

Protecting
Other People's
Children

120 DAYS TO CREATE A STRONG

CHILD SAFETY POLICY

Tom Rawlings & Debbie Ausburn

Hatherleigh Press is committed to preserving and protecting the natural resources of the earth. Environmentally responsible and sustainable practices are embraced within the company's mission statement.

Visit us at www.hatherleighpress.com.

PROTECTING OTHER PEOPLE'S CHILDREN

Library of Congress Cataloging-in-Publication Data is available.
ISBN: 978-1-961293-08-3

Printed in the United States
10 9 8 7 6 5 4 3 2 1

CONTENTS

Introduction: Morality Tales   *ix*

CHAPTER 1:   FALSE ASSUMPTIONS THAT
             UNDERMINE CHILD PROTECTION
             POLICIES   1

CHAPTER 2:   IMPORTANT PRINCIPLES THAT
             KEEP US ON TRACK   13

CHAPTER 3:   CREATING A WORKABLE TIMELINE   25

Worksheets: *Chapters 1–3*   *47*

CHAPTER 4:   FINDING THE RIGHT LEADER
             AND TEAMS   71

CHAPTER 5:   SCREENING ADULTS WHO WORK
             WITH YOUR PROGRAM   81

Worksheets: *Chapters 4–5*   *99*

CHAPTER 6:   CONTROLLING OUTSIDE ACCESS
             TO YOUR PROGRAM   109

CHAPTER 7:   ESTABLISHING BEHAVIOR AND
             BOUNDARY PROTOCOLS   119

CHAPTER 8:   CREATING A STRONG
             SAFETY CULTURE   145

CHAPTER 9:   IMPLEMENTING YOUR CHILD
             PROTECTION POLICY   163

Worksheets: Chapters 6–9   185

CHAPTER 10: RESPONDING TO SERIOUS
             INCIDENTS   191

Worksheets: Chapter 10   215

Conclusion: Wrapping It All Up   221

About the Authors   223

INTRODUCTION:
MORALITY TALES

"Dripping water hollows out stone."

—Ovid

COVERING OVER 1,000 acres in southwest Georgia is
Providence Canyon State Park, a network of sixteen canyons
up to 150 feet deep. It's been dubbed "Georgia's Little Grand
Canyon" for good reason. Erosion has exposed millions of years
of colorful walls of layered sediment. Full of fossils, the lower
walls of the canyon represent sediment laid down over 70 million
years ago.

The entire complex seems ancient. Yet it's less than 200 years
old, the product of poor soil conservation practices in the early
1800s. Farmers stripped the land of trees to produce cotton, failed
to protect the land from runoff, and quickly found their cropland
washed away. You can see smaller versions of Providence Canyon
in the many gullies that dot former cotton pastures across middle Georgia.

Credit: Christopher Baily

Like the farmers who lost their land to erosion, youth-serving organizations have found themselves in situations where small, unaddressed failures to protect their staff and beneficiaries have led to major scandals that threaten the future of the organizations. It's happened in recent years to churches: the Catholic Church, the Southern Baptist Convention, the Anglican Church in North America. It's happened to charitable organizations: Oxfam, Save the Children, the Boy Scouts of America. Each of these organizations has watched its reputation and its future implode from a scandalous crisis that was years in the making. Two high-profile scandals provide some important object lessons.

THE SOUTHERN BAPTIST CONVENTION

The Southern Baptist Convention's (SBC) problems began with inattention to allegations of sexual abuse and harassment within its affiliated churches. It blew up in a series of Houston Chronicle articles from early 2019 under the headline "Abuse of Faith: 20 Years, 700 Victims: Southern Baptist Sexual Abuse Spreads as Leaders Resist Reforms."

The Chronicle's reporting revealed, among other problems, that the denomination had for years avoided addressing claims of sexual abuse by individuals affiliated with Southern Baptist congregations and organizations. The Chronicle series, however, did spur action. Beginning in 2021 as part of its reform efforts, the denomination's Sexual Abuse Task Force commissioned a report on the church's history of addressing sexual abuse. That report dug deeper into victims' efforts to persuade the church to address abuse and concluded that they tried to raise these issues with church leaders over a number of years, but were roundly rebuffed each time.

OXFAM

Oxfam has traditionally been one of the UK's leading charities, with celebrity ambassadors and supporters such as the actress Minnie Driver, Bishop Desmond Tutu, and members of the band, Coldplay. In 2016-17, the poverty-fighting organization raised over €300,000,000—about half of that from government funders.

On February 9, 2018, the *Times of London* published a damning article under the headline "Top Oxfam Staff Paid Haiti Survivors for Sex." Thus began a public relations disaster for the organization, as further articles accused leaders of covering up sexual misconduct not only in Haiti but also in Chad.

The UK regulatory body for charitable organizations, the Charity Commission, issued a bombshell report finding that

Oxfam had long ignored abuse and other wrongdoing in its programs. Going back several years, the Commission found long-standing problems: lack of awareness of standards for behavior; failure to report incidents of sexual abuse; and coddling of staff who committed acts of abuse. "Oxfam's internal culture tolerated poor behaviour, and at times lost sight of the values it stands for," said the Charity Commission's statement.

COMMON DENOMINATORS

Each of these scandals reflects an organizational culture and climate that failed to fulfill the group's mission to protect its beneficiaries and staff. Three glaring flaws stand out from these and other recent scandals.

Policies and Reporting Requirements Ignored

Until recent years, many organizations neglected to put in place appropriate protection policies. The UK's Independent Inquiry into Child Sexual Abuse found that some child-serving organizations had no child protection policies and procedures whatsoever. The UK report also found that many other organizations that did have policies failed to follow them. "Where policies and procedures were in existence, they were often inadequate or not complied with," the study found. "Recommendations made following internal or external reviews were infrequently implemented and sometimes ignored."

A Culture of Fiefdoms

In many of the failure-to-protect scandals, investigators found that organizations had cultures in which certain staff or programs were "above the law." The U.S. Education Department's investigation into Penn State's football program "identified numerous instances where cultural and climate factors in the football program adversely affected campus safety operations, primarily involving the student conduct process." University officials told the department's investigators that there was "a discernible sense among some athletes that the rules did not apply to them equally." Echoes of that culture are found in the SOS International Villages report:

> "For example, in one country the organisational culture was described as 'a kingdom and a family', with most interviewees expressing very strong emotions of fear, anxiety, silence, fear of job loss for speaking out, and feeling powerless. In another country, interviewees described some staff as 'untouchable' and reported a culture of 'cover-up and collusion'. One senior regional manager was, according to an interviewee, 'chosen by the founder, untouchable.'"

A Focus on Reputation Over Mission

The final flaw present in most of these situations is that managers made protecting the organization their highest priority. As the SBC report noted, "Survivors were always viewed through the lens of potential plaintiffs threatening lawsuits, rather than as individuals who had been harmed and were in need of care." This emphasis "created a chilling effect on the ability of the [Executive Committee of the SBC] to be compassionate towards survivors of abuse." Protecting an organization certainly is one valid concern, but it should never be *the* top concern. Your first priority should be carrying out your organization's *total* mission, including all past, present, and future clients.

HOW THIS BOOK CAN HELP

The purpose of this book is to help you avoid each of these pitfalls. We designed our worksheets and explanations to help you develop policies that you can realistically implement to protect the youth in your care. As you work through the exercises, you will learn principles that will enable your organization to develop a robust and sustainable child protection plan, hold everyone accountable, and protect both your program and the minors that it serves.

We've designed worksheets in this book to help you break down the project into manageable tasks and keep up with your progress. If you prefer, you can download all the worksheets using the QR code below.

CHAPTER 1

FALSE ASSUMPTIONS THAT UNDERMINE CHILD PROTECTION POLICIES

The director called in a panic. The police had just left the activity center, responding to reports that a staff member had molested one of the teens who attended there. "I can't believe it," the director said. "He has been one of our best staff members. The kids love him. Parents love him. Families invite him to go on vacation with them. How could this have happened with no one knowing about it?"

MANY OF OUR clients, along with the Catholic Church, the Southern Baptist Convention, the University of Pennsylvania, USA Gymnastics, and countless other organizations, have learned the tragic fact that many things happen in youth-serving organizations (YSOs) that no administrator knows about. In hindsight, we often can see warning signs, and a good plaintiff's lawyer will unearth all of them. Activists will recite them, and reporters will publicize them. But in the rush of running a program and the myriad of tasks we must handle immediately, we simply don't see the danger as it's happening.

Those immediate and urgent pressures make it easy for us to lose sight of the many ways that someone can harm a child in our care. That dynamic is why YSOs need child protection policies. Standardized policies make it automatic for our staff to check vulnerable points, even if they don't have time to think through the reason behind the rule. Child protection policies need to be as automatic as counting heads during swim time or checking harnesses on a zip line. We must weave protection policies solidly into our organization's culture to create sound defenses for our children.

Part of the problem is that we all operate on certain assumptions about our organizations and the people we work with. Making assumptions is not wrong in itself; if we had to continually evaluate every piece of information about our program, we would get so bogged down in perpetual analysis that we would not be able to function. Similarly, if we can't trust the good intentions of our coworkers, we will not be able to work together and our organization will fall apart.

Problems occur when we make the *wrong* assumptions. Many groups operate from a bad set of facts and don't understand the significance of what they are seeing. Those mistakes create opportunities for either accidents or predators. In our experience, several false assumptions crop up again and again, particularly in youth organizations. Until you recognize and counter these assumptions, there is no child protection policy that will work for you.

"WE COPIED A GREAT POLICY"

Because YSO administrators have so many things to do, it is very tempting to just copy a child protection policy from another organization. There also are many comprehensive programs that you can buy. The problem with this approach is that there is no one-size-fits-all policy. No matter how outstanding the policy is, if you merely adopt it without thinking through the underlying principles and how they apply to your organization's resources, the policy simply will not work. There are too many variations among YSOs. A policy that works well for an overnight camp likely will not work as well for a mentoring organization or group home. Some protocols, such as screening, might work while others, such as supervision ratios, will not. Similarly, interaction rules for a group home serving teenagers will be completely different from those for a childcare center. For organizations working in multiple states or countries, the differences between each jurisdiction's laws and regulations adds another layer of difficulty.

Another problem with copying a policy wholesale is that, if it doesn't fit well, you won't be able to implement it consistently. It may be too ambitious for your resources or simply will not work for your staffing arrangements. A policy that you don't follow is, in the world of risk management, worse than no policy at all. If disaster strikes, the media and the courts will hold you to the standards that you set for yourself. Every aspect of the policy that you could not implement will become a way to hold your YSO liable for the tragedy.

Furthermore, your YSO may face different areas of risk than other groups. A childcare center, for example, needs to watch for children biting each other, not online bullying. Similarly, a "no touch" policy can cause emotional harm to younger children but be reassuring to teenagers. Sexual abuse is always a high-impact risk, but careless accidents are more common. You need to do your own individual cost-benefit analysis of various policies and determine the greatest risks that your YSO faces. Those high-risk areas are where you need to allocate your resources.

For all these reasons, this book will rarely recommend a particular protocol. We believe that it is far better for you to learn the principles of a good child protection policy and then apply those principles to your particular YSO. The process will take more time this way, but it will give you a policy that you can implement and enforce consistently.

"PROTECTING THE ORGANIZATION SHOULD NOT BE A PRIORITY"

The lawyer leaned over the table toward the witness. "Ms. Jones," he said menacingly, "Are you telling me that one of your goals in setting up a policy was to protect your organization?" The administrator stammered and struggled to explain. "That's OK," the lawyer said as he leaned back. "I think we understand your motivations. No more questions."

This nightmare scenario is not an unusual one. People who work with YSOs by and large are good-hearted people used to making sacrifices for others. It feels and sounds wrong to say that we want to protect our organization, as though having that goal somehow diminishes our concern for children.

That hesitation is the wrong way to view child protection policies. Of course, our primary goal should be to protect the children in our care. But we also need to protect our organizations. After all, if the organization fails, then all the good that it accomplishes will fail along with it. The children you serve will no longer have your group as a resource. Even if they can find other groups, the unnecessary disruption will be hard for them. We should not apologize for the mission of our organization or the good that it accomplishes. Protecting its ability to carry out its mission is a noble goal that we should claim with pride. Our mission is to protect past, present, *and* future clients.

Protecting the organization's mission also includes protecting its staff from false accusations. While research shows that most reports from children are true, we know that children do misunderstand situations or even lie. A mistaken accusation can take down a staff member and your organization as surely as a truthful one. Good child protection policies will enable an adult to prove, for example, that he or she only interacted with a child when others were nearby or in a room with windows and an open door. Solid protocols serve to protect not only your organization's children, but also its staff and volunteers.

So, if you ever find yourself in Ms. Jones' nightmare or called upon to justify your policies to a governing board or critic, do not hesitate to claim the high ground. Be confident in the vital services that your YSO provides to your clients. Be proud of your role in providing those services. Protecting your organization should never be your *top* priority, but there is no shame in keeping it as *one of* the priorities of your policies.

"WE ARE ON THE ALERT FOR PEDOPHILES"

Another mistake that many YSOs make is concentrating all their efforts on preventing sexual predators from entering the organization. While hardening your organization against pedophiles is an important goal, placing too much emphasis there can distract from other equally important concerns.

First, there is no foolproof way to "detect" sexual predators. They are almost uncanny in their ability to lull suspicions and avoid discovery. As more than one of our clients has said, "Until we heard the molestation charges, we thought he was the best worker we had ever had."

Researchers working with sex offenders have been able to identify some common characteristics, but many of them become apparent only in hindsight. We simply don't see them in the day-to-day activities of our YSO. Until we see how the story ends, we don't understand the significance of the clues scattered along the way.

Focusing on pedophile characteristics sweeps in a lot of innocent people. We naturally tend to revert to whatever stereotype we have in our heads. We tag the creepy old guy at the park as a pedophile though in reality, he might just be a lonely person with few social skills.

We can play it safe with the creepy old man, as avoiding him only costs us the opportunity to connect with another human being. In our YSOs, however, responding to a false positive can cost us a good staff member who could help our children. For example, mental health research consistently shows that one of the best ways that children can overcome trauma is to have a mentor. Thus, one of the best services we can provide those children is to connect them with a caring mentor. However, many commonly cited signs of grooming for sexual abuse mimic virtues we look for in good mentors. Spending time with kids, listening to them, and bonding with them are all characteristics of both top-notch mentors and sexual predators.

If, out of an excess of caution, we exclude a caring adult who could help the children in our program, then we lose a resource for those kids. Our clients continually tell us about the difficulty in finding good staff and volunteers for their programs. Stringent rules weed out both pedophiles and good people who just do not have time to deal with the requirements and the risk of false accusations.

A second problem with focusing on sexual predators is that, while sexual abuse may get all the headlines, it is far from the only way that children can be harmed. Other forms of abuse and simple accidents harm far more children every year. We have seen many times that staff in childcare centers, for example, have accidentally pulled a child's arm, resulting in an injury so common that it has been known for centuries as "nursemaid's elbow." Physical abuse, both reckless and deliberate, is far more common than sexual abuse, and emotional abuse is more common than either. Not only are these problems more common, but the injuries can be just as devastating. The parents of a child injured in a hazing incident will not be comforted to know that no sexual predators worked in your organization.

A comprehensive child protection policy must include all the harms and injuries that a child risks while in your care. If yours is a high adventure camp, then the safety rules for your ropes course are part of your child protection policy. If your group transports kids in a bus or individual cars, then your screening protocol for the drivers is part of your child protection policy.

Listing every safety rule for every program that you might have is beyond the scope of this book. Our point is simply that you need to keep a broad perspective on the potential risks to children in your care. You know better than anyone else the details of your programs and the safety rules that you need. Don't focus so exclusively on screening out sexual predators that you forget to screen out bad drivers, ill-tempered physical abusers, or opportunistic adults.

"WE ARE KEEPING A CLOSE EYE ON ADULTS"

Another common misconception is that YSO child protection policies should address only dangers from malicious adults. Multiple statistics, however, show that youth are more likely to victimize other youth, either sexually, physically, or emotionally, than are adults. You need to protect your clients from each other as much as from predatory adults.

It's not just deliberate harm that we need to keep in mind. All of us who work with children know that they are not born with good judgment. Until their brains develop sufficiently (sometime in their 20s), they simply cannot understand all the ramifications of their decisions. So, we must protect them from both their own and their peers' bad judgment. Practical jokes, enthusiasm, and ineptness all can spiral into serious injuries.

Keeping this principle in mind will help you avoid several mistakes that we have seen many YSOs make. For example, some overnight camps, concerned about the possibility of sexual abuse from counselors, changed their sleeping arrangements to place all the counselors in the same dorm room. The theory was that the counselors could keep an eye on each other, thereby preventing any nighttime abuse. Of course, the arrangement also left the campers with no adult supervision. In all those camps, a few practical jokes gone awry—fortunately with no serious injuries—convinced them to switch back to placing adults in each room. The camp couldn't ignore the risk of sexual abuse, but it had to find a different solution than leaving minors unsupervised.

Your YSO will have similar dilemmas. It is impossible to completely avoid risk; you can only reduce it. Harm from adults is a high-impact risk, but harm from other children is a more likely one. Be sure that your child protection policies address both.

"WE KNOW EVERYONE"

Smaller YSOs tend to rely on a small group of people and to believe that they can trust each other implicitly. That trust makes it all too easy for someone to slip through any safeguards and harm a child. To some extent, the flaw is built into the way that small organizations work. With limited manpower, you cannot watch everyone all the time. You must trust each other in order to function. Unfortunately, we can never truly know everything about someone else or see their hidden motives. We have seen too many small organizations devastated by someone who recklessly or maliciously abused their trust.

A good child protection policy can help avoid this pitfall, at least in the area of harm to children. It becomes a matter of consistent routine, not trust or distrust. If you adopt a good policy that you can consistently enforce, then you can apply it to everyone from Board members to volunteers. You do not have to second-guess yourself or worry about reading someone's mind. Pedophiles generally take the path of least resistance; if you enforce rules that make it difficult for them, they will seek out a different group. If your staff consistently follows rules about safety, workers are less likely to make careless mistakes that enable predators.

Small organizations sometimes resist child protection policies because they can be expensive and time-consuming, at least initially. It is much easier to just roll along, relying on the trust that you have in each other. You may be right; not every adult will take advantage of your trust. But you are taking an incredible risk when you operate on that assumption.

Furthermore, instituting a child protection policy will give dividends far beyond lowering your risk. If you follow the principles in this book, you will come out with a much more professional organization on many levels, and one that is much more flexible in avoiding problems. It will take time and commitment, but your organization will be far stronger at the end of the process.

"WE HAVE A GREAT POLICY... SOMEWHERE AROUND HERE"

As we mentioned before, the worst policy you can have from a risk/reward perspective is one that you don't enforce. If you have adopted or bought a program that ended up just sitting on a shelf, then you have wasted your resources and created a huge risk for your YSO. If disaster strikes, you will find yourself explaining endlessly why the YSO was not following the ambitious policy that it adopted.

This problem is why your policy needs to be in line with your YSO's resources. If you lack the manpower to call four references and 3 former employers for every job applicant, then don't include that goal in your policy. Limit your calls to people who pass a second interview or lower the number of references you require. If you cannot realistically control access to your group, such as field trips or sports teams that play in public venues, then don't include screening all adults in your policy. Instead, focus on supervision and ensure that you have the staff and volunteers you need to adequately supervise your group in public settings.

It is good to set goals for your YSO. In this instance, however, don't make them ambitious. Be realistic about what you can achieve and how you can allocate your resources. It's better to exceed your own goals than to fall short.

As you work through this book, be aware of your assumptions and how they affect your child protection policies. What we are asking you to do may take a bit more time than simply copying policies from a handbook, but the process will be far more effective in the end. The goal is for you to develop a realistic, customized, and enforceable policy that becomes a seamless part of the myriad of ways that you serve children.

CHAPTER 2

IMPORTANT PRINCIPLES THAT KEEP US ON TRACK

YOU'RE PROBABLY THINKING, "OK, I get that I need to change my assumptions. But what do I change them *to?*" That's what this chapter is about. This workbook is built on several important principles that underlie every good child protection policy. The goal of this book is for your child protection policy to become an integral part of your program's culture. To reach that goal, you need to follow the following six important principles as you develop your procedures.

#1: UNDERSTAND THE DIFFERENCE BETWEEN PRINCIPLES, POLICIES, AND PROCEDURES

A recurrent problem we see is child protection or safeguarding policies that conflate *principles* of child protection with *policies and procedures* for child protection. These documents are often a mix of specific actions that employees must take or avoid and ideals that employees must uphold. Mixed among the principles and policies, you'll often find prohibitions on actions that don't themselves constitute child abuse, neglect, or exploitation but are included to *prevent* abuse and exploitation. The result can be a confusing set of directives that are hard for your organization to follow.

Let's take an example from the public child safeguarding policy of a prominent child-serving organization. While this organization (which will remain nameless) has a more detailed internal policy, this public statement shows some of the typical flaws we see in many policies:

[YSO] is Committed to Children

[YSO] is committed to conducting its programs and operations in a manner that is safe for the children it serves and to helping protect the children with whom [YSO] is in contact.

1. *Representatives are explicitly prohibited from engaging in any activity that may result in any kind of Child Abuse.*

2. *Representatives are expected to create and proactively maintain an environment that aims to prevent and deter any actions and omissions, whether deliberate or inadvertent, that place children at risk of any kind of Child Abuse.*

3. *Any violations of this policy will be treated as a serious infraction and will result in disciplinary action being taken, up to and including termination and any other available legal remedy.*

4. *Representatives must at all times avoid actions that could be construed to constitute potentially abusive behavior;*

representatives must never place themselves in a position
where they are made vulnerable to allegations of misconduct.

5. *[YSO] has adopted Procedures, described below, to promote*
    training and prevention, reporting, responding.

This policy fails to separate intentional wrongdoing from human error and fails to distinguish incidents in which a child suffers harm from risky practices. The policy stresses that "[a]ny violations of this policy will be treated as a serious infraction and will result in disciplinary action . . ." While it's great that the organization takes child protection seriously, it's doubtful that it will punish *all* violations of policy. Exactly when and how will the YSO cite an employee for failing to "create and proactively maintain an environment" that is safe for children? Or for "engaging in any activity that may result in any kind of Child Abuse"?

The organization elsewhere defines "child abuse" as "anything which individuals, institutions or processes do or fail to do which directly or indirectly harms children or damages their prospect of safe and healthy development into adulthood." Under this policy, the mere fact that a child suffers an injury could be cause for discipline even if the employee did his or her best to protect the child. Furthermore, the policy gives management the discretion to determine in hindsight whether the environment or activity was safe for children. The only way to implement this policy is to create an environment of micromanaging, arbitrary enforcement, and terrible employee morale. That's not a culture that will actually protect children.

Here's another example we often see. It's common to have a list of "thou shalt nots" that, while certainly clear and detailed, are not always a good basis for discipline.

Every member of [YSO] must:

1. *Never be alone with a child, whether in a room or outside.*

2. *Keep all rooms used by adults and minors accessible (no locked doors) and with open visibility.*

3. *Never go somewhere with a child that could appear isolated.*

4. *Always be within sight and close proximity to others.*

5. *Never solicit physical contact from children.*

6. *Always be cautious and aware of any issues.*

7. *Never let children sit on their lap, or allow children to lay their heads or hands on their lap.*

8. *Never give front hugs, piggyback rides, or touch under the shoulders.*

9. *Never go into a restroom at the same time as a child.*

10. *Not leave children unsupervised while under the care of [YSO].*

11. *Report all suspicious or inappropriate behavior to the director or leader of [YSO] camps and investigation will commence immediately.*

These rules certainly are clear and detailed, but they don't seem to have any unifying principle, and they don't consider many contexts in which these actions are beneficial to children. Should a day camp worker refuse to have a five-year old sit in her lap if that child is seeking comfort after falling on the playground and hurting her knee? Of course not. It also matters if the incident is occurring in a group where there are other adults present, or happening while the adult and child are alone in an office. If the list started with a positive principle stating that workers need to recognize and meet children's needs in an appropriate and healthy manner, it would set the important context for the general rules and any exceptions.

As you are working through the auditing and drafting steps outlined in this book, keep in mind that you need to first establish the principles of your program. Educational institutions may have principles of providing exemplary instruction for young people or meeting their learning needs in an appropriate and emotionally healthy manner. High adventure programs may have the principle of teaching youth how to safely learn skills and challenge their emotional and physical limits. Your program's principles will be unique to your organization, but whatever they are, you first need to set them out. Then, you can work out how those principles show up in policies and practices.

#2: KNOW THE STANDARDS IN YOUR FIELD

You must know the standards in your field for child protection policies. You will find those standards in several distinct places:

Licensing and Regulatory Standards

If state or federal regulations govern your industry, then those rules will set the minimum standards that you must follow. For example, most childcare centers must have state licenses and follow licensing rules. If those licensing rules require three (3) reference checks before hiring someone, then your standard is at least three (3) checks. You have no choice but to find room in your schedule to do those checks, no matter what your other sources of standards recommend. Similarly, Title IX applies to all school programs (including K–12) that receive government funds. Complying with Title IX regulations, then, is a baseline for child protection policies in any such school.

Finally, licensing rules for other organizations in your field may establish a legal concept called the "standard of care." That phrase has different meanings in different states, but generally it means the standard that most organizations in your field follow. So even if the rules don't directly apply to your organization, they may set standards that you still need to follow. For example, many states exempt church nurseries from regulations for childcare centers. Yet, the regulations may still establish the standard of care because they have become the norm for child-caring programs. So be aware of the regulations that govern other organizations in your field, even if they don't apply directly to you.

Association Standards

Many industries have organizations where participation is voluntary, but the standards are mandatory for members. Safe Sport for youth sporting programs is one such example. Safe Sport rules apply to most national sports organizations, and any local sports program that wants to participate in those organizations must follow Safe Sport guidelines. Because Safe Sport is so well-known, its policies have become the default standard even for many groups that are not part of those national programs. As with regulations, these voluntary policies can become part of the standard of care in a field.

Accreditation Standards

Accreditation is another voluntary standard that offers guidance. Different accreditation associations have different rules that help you meet the standard in the industry. You can find this in National Association for the Education of Young Children (NAEYC) for childcare centers or the American Camping Association (ACA) for camping programs or any number of education programs. Because these accreditation standards are voluntary, they aren't mandatory standards for the industry, but they may offer good information about what most of the groups in your industry are doing.

Guidelines and Publications

As we mentioned earlier, there are numerous books and paid programs about child protection policies. While we don't recommend that you simply *adopt* someone else's program, these publications are excellent sources of information that you can *adapt* to your organization. One excellent resource that is a bit dated but still has timeless recommendations is the CDC publication, *Preventing Child Sexual Abuse Within Youth-Serving Organizations: Getting Started With Policies and Procedures*, available at www.cdc.gov. Its principles work well for preventing all types of abuse, not only sexual abuse.

Many insurance companies publish recommendations, either in formal publications or in informal blog posts or emails. Ask your insurance agent not only whether your insurer has such publications, but what other insurance companies work in your field. Those other companies are likely to have publications on their websites that can give you some helpful ideas.

Custom and Practice in Your Area

A final important source of standards is the policies of other organizations similar to yours in your geographic area. You will need to keep up with developments in your field and pay attention as customs change. For example, for many years, no one thought about criminal record checks for volunteers. However, the practice is so common now that all organizations that work with young people need to do some level of checks for volunteers who have access to young people. Even if statutes or licensing rules don't require you to conduct those checks, the fact that everyone else does means that your program also must meet that standard.

#3: IF IT'S NOT WRITTEN DOWN, IT DOESN'T EXIST

Many of our clients have found themselves in trouble because they relied on informal practices rather than written policies. Relying on custom instead of written policies leaves several holes in your child protection practices. First, not everyone will hear about unwritten policies. We've all been in situations where we learned after the fact "that's not how we do it here." Even if you have an orientation session for new workers, it's all too easy to forget one policy or another. The only way to be sure that you have communicated all your policies is to put them in writing.

Second, it's hard to enforce unwritten policies. In most states, you will have a hard time disciplining or firing employees unless you can point to a written policy that clearly sets out expectations. Even if you can discipline a worker for violating an unwritten procedure, you'll face the claim that your enforcement is arbitrary and selective.

Finally, if someone makes a claim against your program, you will not be able to prove what an unwritten policy required. Workers' memories of such policies tend to vary wildly, and everyone will have their own version of what they thought the policy was. The only way to prove that you had a particular requirement in place is to be able to point to a written document.

As you work through your child protection policies, be sure that you learn about any unwritten practices that your employees are following. If the procedures are good ones, then include them in your written policies. If the practices are problematic, then you need to close any loopholes in your written policy and concentrate on training your workers to follow that written policy. One of your primary goals during the processes we outline in this book is to be sure that what your workers are actually doing aligns with your written policies.

#4: ONLY WRITE DOWN WHAT YOU CAN DO

Another important aspect of written policies is to be sure that they reflect what you actually are able to do, not what you hope you can do someday. Aspirations are wonderful, but child protection policies are not the place for them. If someone makes a claim against you, your jurisdiction may hold you responsible for everything you put in writing, including hopes and dreams. Be sure that your policy only includes what you can do.

Be brutally honest in this respect. If you do not have the manpower to conduct more references than the usual standard for your industry, then don't set that high standard. Write down the lower standard. You can always conduct more references when you have the resources. It's always better to exceed your written standards than to fall short.

Also, be certain that you can follow your policy consistently and impartially. Sporadic or arbitrary compliance with a given procedure isn't any better than ignoring it completely. Your child protection policy needs to become an integral part of your organizations' culture, and the only way for that to happen is for everyone to learn how to consistently do what the policy calls for.

#5: WEAVE POLICIES THROUGHOUT YOUR PROGRAM

A child protection policy should not be a single standalone component of your program. Just as child protection involves more than prohibiting only pedophiles victimizing children, your policies need to address more than one type of problem. The strongest policies are those that permeate every aspect of your organization's culture. Thus, be sure that your policies to protect children show up in as many places as possible in your documentation and training.

Some placements will be obvious. Rules about how adults treat minors should be in your staff handbooks or agreements, while rules about interactions between minors should be in documents addressed to them. Look for other places where you can post pieces or summaries of your child protection policies. In policies about teachers' free periods, for example, repeat any restrictions you have about keeping doors open. If yours is a mentoring organization, repeat applicable policies about transportation or one-to-one contact whenever you send emails about group activities or planned events. The more often you can remind everyone about how your policies apply to ordinary activities, the more the policies will become part of your everyday practices and culture.

#6: ADAPT, DON'T ADOPT

Finally, in reviewing your own programs and policies, avoid the trap of adopting someone else's policies without thoroughly analyzing them. If you simply copy another organization's policies, it is unlikely that you can make it part of your program's unique culture. The "adapt, don't adopt" rule doesn't mean that you must reinvent the wheel. There's no problem with borrowing liberally from work that someone else already has done. Simply be sure that you are reviewing the policies and adapting them to your program's unique needs, paying particular attention to the following factors.

Look for specific policies. It's not enough to have a set of policies; the organization must also ensure that those policies reasonably address all the risks that are common to programs serving children and youth. In this chapter, we've given an outline of policies that you need to consider.

Test any new policies. Have you tested out your written policies in real life? Don't fall into the trap of going with a policy that only sounds good. Test it in limited circumstances, or at least do a tabletop exercise to think through how it will work in your organization. When you audit your policies, pay particular attention to the newest policies and how they worked in actual practice.

Train your staff. Be sure that your staff and volunteers know what's in your policies. Failing to ensure that your workers abide by your policies can be worse than not having any. More importantly, listen to what your workers say about whether the policies are working in practice. Your frontline staff and workers will know far sooner than any administrators of problems in written policies. Use their feedback to ensure that your written policies will work consistently for your program.

As you work through the timeline and exercises in this book, keep the above six principles in mind. Refer back to them as you audit, write, and tweak your child protection policies. They are essential parts of creating a culture in your organization that makes child protection an instinctive process for everyone involved.

CHAPTER 3

CREATING A WORKABLE TIMELINE

"I'm overwhelmed," the school principal complained. "I have to deal with curriculum, student discipline, HR problems, disgruntled parents, and the Board. Now I have to create new child protection policies, and I had to do it yesterday. I simply can't find the time to get it all done."

MOST ADMINISTRATORS HAVE this reaction to yet more advice about child protection policies. It seems that you must do it all, and do it right now. That's why we have organized this book to give you a timeline of tasks. We concentrate on workable action steps that you can juggle with the rest of your responsibilities within a manageable time frame. Taking one step at a time, you can have at the end of the process a solid child protection policy that will work for your organization.

This chapter outlines our recommended timeline. We include deadlines, on the theory that people need deadlines to help focus on tasks, but they are soft deadlines. Use them as targets, knowing that, like everything else involved in creating a strong child protection policy, you should adapt our recommendations to your unique situation.

Finally, use the worksheets included here to work through the process. We designed them with the aim of helping you break down the project into manageable tasks and keep up with your progress.

The bird's-eye view of the timeline is below, and the rest of the chapter expands on each phase. The remaining chapters in the book give in-depth descriptions of each task. Together, the book and the worksheets will guide you to a solid child protection policy, one step at a time.

Many people prefer to have a separate notebook of the worksheets. If you would like separate copies to create your own notebook, you can download all the worksheets at ProtectingOtherPeoplesChildren.com/download-checklist.

Bird's-Eye View of The Timeline

First 30 Days	
	Name a Child Safety Coordinator (CSC), Child Safety Team (CST), and Incident Response Team (IRT)
	Confirm that your organization has committed to giving the CSC resources and support
	Be sure your governing documents communicate how your child protection policy is grounded in the organization's mission and culture
	Ensure governing documents reflect a commitment to child safety
	Research and develop definition of child maltreatment (both CST & IRT)
	Complete initial audit of your current policies (CST)
	Audit current insurance policy (IRT)
	Begin locating past insurance policies (IRT)
First 60–90 Days	
	Audit employee files for criminal records checks (CRCs), conduct any missing CRCs (CST)
	Start locating additional insurance coverage if needed (IRT)
	Develop child protection policies (CST)
	Develop incident response policies (IRT)

First 120–150 Days	
	Audit all records for all employees, volunteers, and interns; re-screen as needed to meet new standards (CST)
	Board audits itself for good governance standards
	Develop additional non-core policies (CST & IRT)
	Training for all workers in mandated reporter responsibilities (IRT)
	Training for all workers in new child protection policies (CST)
	Consider training for children and parents (CST)
	Specialized training for people screening employees and volunteers
	Consider upgrades to physical facility, develop budget and timeline for feasible changes
Yearly and Ongoing	
	Audit worker files and fill in missing CRCs and reference checks
	Survey employees
	Review incident reports
	Assess whether policies are working or need changes

FIRST 30 DAYS: TEAMS, PHILOSOPHY, AND AUDITS

The first 30 days of your work sets the foundation for your child protection policy. Spend this time investigating standards and evaluating your current policies. With the two exceptions explained below, don't worry yet about writing new policies or changing existing ones. That project will come later, after you know what you have and what you need.

The first essential step is to pull together the teams who will do the work. After that, the teams can take the following tasks in any order. However, be certain that the teams do all the investigation and evaluation required *before* they start actually writing or tweaking policies.

The following chapters in this book explain in detail the principles you need in your child protection policy. For now, we'll just summarize what you'll find on the worksheets. Use the details in the following chapters to know what you should be looking for in this initial phase.

Coordinator and Teams

Your first step is to bring your teams together. Your Child Safety and Incident Response teams will work with you throughout this process and help you with your policies. We recommend teams for several reasons. First, having groups working together helps spread the load around. Second, getting other people involved allows you to get multiple perspectives and areas of expertise. Finally, these team members will help your organization make child protection an ongoing part of the mission rather than a one-time project.

The jobs of these teams are not finished once they write the policies. They shouldn't just write a policy that you will stick on a shelf—the team members should also help enforce and continually evaluate the policies. These teams will help make child protection a living part of your culture.

PAID CONSULTANTS

We often have clients ask us about using paid consultants to develop child protection policies. We don't object to consultants (indeed, we offer that service ourselves). Consultants certainly can offer subject matter expertise and they can be unparalleled resources for evaluating and/or writing policies. They cannot substitute, however, for a team that stays involved long term. If you decide to use consultants, make sure that they are teaching principles to your team, not just dictating policies. Also, ensure that the work the consultants do is the start of your process, not the end point.

Child Safety Coordinator

The point person will be the Child Safety Coordinator (CSC), who usually is the leader of both teams. We recommend one person to lead both teams so that your organization has someone with a high-level view of all the work that's happening. This person needs to be not only a leader, but someone with the authority to implement and enforce policies.

Child Safety Team

The first team we recommend is the Child Safety Team (CST). This group will be responsible for evaluating, writing, and following up on the bulk of your improved child protection policy. Most of this team's work will be in the first 30–120 days of evaluating and creating or tweaking policies. This group also needs to continually evaluate how the organization is carrying out its responsibility of protecting children. So choose members who are willing to make an ongoing commitment to the project.

Incident Response Teams

The Incident Response Team (IRT) deals with injuries and significant violations of policy. Most people assume that the IRT only needs to be involved after a serious incident. We recommend that this team start its work much earlier, from the beginning of the process, both to help avoid policy violations and to be better prepared if and when incidents happen.

PHILOSOPHY AND DEFINITION

Now we come to the only actual writing that you need to do during the first 30 days. First, your CSC and CST need to work with your governing Board or owners to embed the importance of child protection in your organization's foundation documents. Second, both teams and the CSC need to develop a workable definition of child maltreatment that will inform all your policies and practices.

Philosophy

A solid child protection policy shows up in every part of an organization's work, starting with both governing and aspirational documents. Evaluate your organization's mission statement, by-laws, founding documents, and website statements. Do they reflect the importance of protecting the children in your care? If not, work with your Board or C-Suite to write that philosophy into the documents.

Doing this task within the first 30 days ensures that your decision makers understand the importance of child protection and are willing to make the changes needed to strengthen your policies. If you can't get these changes made in your organization's foundational documents, then you need to back up and be sure that everyone is on board before you start spending time developing policies that the organization isn't actually interested in enacting.

There is no particular language that's best for these documents. We recommend, though, that your child protection philosophy include language reflecting most of the following points:

1. **Describe child safety as a key goal.** Your organization needs to keep child safety as a central tenet, not simply one of several good outcomes.

2. **If your organization has a particular religious or philosophical foundation, list what those source documents say about child safety.** For example, Christian organizations should include Bible verses about the responsibility to protect children. Other religious organizations should refer to the texts that underpin their religious beliefs, while secular

organizations should refer to their philosophical foundations. Whatever your organization's particular perspective, cite the philosophical or religious sources that govern it.

3. **Incorporate a longer explanation somewhere of what child safety means to your organization.** You don't have to include all the details every time the topic comes up; summaries are fine in shorter documents, such as mission statements. Just be sure that there is a comprehensive explanation somewhere in your governing documents.

Every organization has its own unique mission and goals. Within the first 30 days, locate or write language in your foundational documents that reflects the priority of child protection. Then use those statements as your goalposts as you evaluate and strengthen your policies.

Definitions of Maltreatment

While you are developing your philosophy, your CSC, the safety team, and the response team need to develop definitions of child maltreatment. This is not the place for an aspirational statement of child dignity or flourishing. Those are good goals, but they belong elsewhere. What you need for these definitions is concrete, workable language that will enable everyone in your program to recognize maltreatment when they see it.

For example, a common definition of physical abuse is "non-accidental injury." It's clear, short, and easily recognizable. People can remember it without having to look back into a handbook. If it's in line with your state's laws and regulations, that phrase could be part of your organization's definition of physical abuse.

That phrase illustrates another fact about your definition, which is that you shouldn't have a single phrase or sentence to cover all the different kinds of abuse. You will need a definition of physical abuse, for example, and a definition of bullying. The teams should draft definitions to cover all the different types of maltreatment that your organization needs to avoid internally and recognize externally.

The relevant types of maltreatment will vary according to your jurisdiction and your client base. Summer camps, for example, rarely need to worry about school truancy laws. Your teams need to review all the categories of maltreatment to decide what is relevant to your organization. We set out the most common types of maltreatment in our discussion of mandated reporter laws in Chapter 10. Use the details there to help inform your definitions.

Be particularly careful when defining amorphous concepts such as bullying or emotional abuse. It's very easy for definitions to confuse bullying and ordinary conflict, for example, and it's important to know the difference. Not everything that makes a child sad is bullying or emotional abuse. Learning how to deal with conflict and hurt feelings are important life skills for children, and we do not serve them well by buffering them from those situations to the point of eliminating these critical lessons. Avoid open-ended aspirational definitions that lend themselves to arbitrary enforcement. Look for clear definitions with objective measures.

Finally, your definitions do not have to include every detail. Whether your state's child pornography laws cover teen sexting, for example, is probably a better topic for training events. What you should strive for is a definition that allows people to recognize the possibility immediately and start asking more questions.

Saying that physical abuse is "non-accidental injury," for example, does not answer the question of what's an accident or whether a non-permanent red mark on a child's skin is an injury. Nevertheless, the definition is a good one, not because it covers every detail, but because it's short enough to be memorable and provide a concrete framework for more questions.

Where to Find Definitions

There are several places that your teams can look for help in drafting these definitions.

State laws and regulations. This is the first stop for your teams. Any definition you have must match what your state or licensing authority requires. Your IRT, the team responsible for dealing with mandated reporter responsibilities during this project, should ensure that your definition also matches child protection and mandated reporter statutes. In this respect, you will have a minimum standard for defining maltreatment.

Associations and accreditation. Look at the definitions of your accrediting bodies and associations that you have joined. Even if you don't have to follow those definitions, they can offer excellent resources for your teams.

Teaching and awareness organizations. Other organizations that work in a particular field can offer helpful guidance. For example, both the CDC and stopbullying.gov offer workable definitions of bullying. Some groups may be too ideological or too opposed to your group's foundational beliefs for you to adopt their complete definitions, but most of them can offer at least some helpful ideas to consider.

Initial Audit

Spend the rest of your first 30 days auditing your policies. You can't figure out what you need to write until you know what you already have. This is the beginning of a collaborative process with your teams to develop policies that your organization can implement consistently. The worksheets and the following chapters give details about what you should be looking for in each aspect of the audits.

We recommend that the IRT evaluate your (1) whistleblower policies; (2) mandated reporter policies; (3) mandated reporter training; (4) insurance coverage and historic policies; (5) document retention policies; and (6) communications policies. All these areas relate to responding to violations of policies, and we explain them more thoroughly in Chapters 8 and 10. Solid policies in each of those areas are essential to professional and proactive responses in your organization.

The CST should evaluate all the remaining policies: (1) employee and volunteer screening (Chapter 5); (2) access control (Chapter 6); (3) behavior and boundary guidelines (Chapter 7); (4) creating a safety culture (Chapter 8), and (5) planning how your organization will implement its policies (Chapter 9).

Staff Surveys

Both teams should evaluate how your organization implements its child protection policies, as we detailed in this chapter. The best place to start in these first 30 days is to survey staff and perhaps volunteers about their perspectives on how the organization works.

We've included two recommended surveys in Worksheets #3 and #4 that you should consider circulating among stakeholders *before* creating and implementing your policies. As we explain in later chapters, building an organization that protects children and youth requires both good policies and good implementation. Good implementation requires having staff that understand your policies, believe the policies are important, and feel empowered to speak up when others don't follow those policies. The surveys on positive accountability and psychological safety can give you an idea of the current state of your organizational culture and help you understand how to better empower your workers.

FIRST 60 TO 90 DAYS

In the next stage of the process, you start building on the foundation you established in the previous exercise. This is the phase when you start writing or editing your policies to bring them up to the standards you identified in the first 30 days. We also recommend that you use this time to start an in-depth audit of your employee and volunteer files to ensure that they meet your new standards.

The worksheet for this phase is Worksheet #5. You will find detailed recommendations explaining each task in the following chapters of this book.

Audit of Employee and Volunteer Files

At some point in building a strong safety policy, you will need to be sure that your current staff and volunteers meet all your screening standards and that you have the documentation in each file. It's a time-consuming task, and you need to decide on your screening standards first. For that reason, we recommend that you do the bulk of that individual file review in the final phase of this child protection project. However, criminal record checks are a non-negotiable standard, and your safety team can review files for that requirement relatively quickly.

For that reason, we recommend that within the first 60–90 days you (1) decide what criminal records checks (CRCs) to require for which positions, and (2) review the files of your current employees and volunteers to ensure you have documentation of clear records. You may find the screening standards in Worksheet #8 to be helpful for the first task.

If you are missing clear CRCs for anyone who has regular access to children, then get those checks done immediately. To the extent possible, restrict those employees or volunteers from unsupervised access to children while you are awaiting the results of the criminal records checks. In this context, remember that if you cannot find the documentation, then it doesn't exist. Don't rely on your memory; be sure that the file has written documents.

Also note which CRCs are older than five years. As we explain in Chapter 5, you need to periodically recheck the criminal records. Part of your task during these 60–90 days will be to determine how often you need to refresh those CRCs. The longest time period we recommend is five to eight years. If you note the dates in this initial review, you will be able to start with a subset of your records for rechecking once you decide what time frame works for your organization.

Also be sure that, if the existing or new CRCs show a criminal conviction, child maltreatment registry determination, or bad reference check, you have a written explanation in the file of why you decided that record doesn't show that the worker poses a danger to children. As we explain in Chapter 5, not all convictions or arrests or placement on child maltreatment registries will disqualify someone from working in your organization. But if you decide to allow that person to work with children, or to do so with limitations, be sure that the file documents your reasoning.

Write Your Policies

By the time you finish the research and evaluation that we recommend for the first 30 days, you should have a good idea of what you need in your child protection policies. We recommend that the IRT work on the policies that it evaluated. Similarly, the CST should be working on the remaining policies.

As you write the policies, you need to keep some important principles in mind:

Feasibility (Worksheet #6). Your policies must be feasible for your organization. We hope the Feasibility Analysis worksheet will help you think through what to include in a particular policy. If your policy, or a particular detail of it, doesn't get a high score on this analysis, you may just be spinning your wheels. This principle is one reason that it is good to have a variety of perspectives on your two teams. Get everyone's input on whether the policies that you are considering actually will work in your organization.

Building a safety culture (Chapter 8). You are not creating just another policy for your organization; you are building a child safety culture. As you develop your policies, follow the principles we discuss in Chapter 2. Analyze and learn from the stakeholder surveys that you conducted in the first 30 days.

Developing a strong safety culture requires developing clear and just consequences for policy violations. You must avoid both permissive attitudes that allow incompetent or malevolent people to remain in your program and draconian consequences that expel good people and hurt morale. As you develop your policies, use Worksheet #11 and the principles in Chapter 2 to craft consequences that will help you build a just and safe culture for employees and minors.

FIRST 120 DAYS

After you've written your core policies, it's time to draft less urgent policies and finish time-consuming audits. It's also the time to start implementing your new safety culture by communicating your policies to your employees and stakeholders.

Board or Ownership

Now is a good time to encourage your Board to audit itself for good governance standards. Governing boards, like any other group, are subject to inertia and just as prone to overlook maintenance in the urgency of day-to-day matters. Now that your organization, including the Board, is looking at the policies involved in child protection, it's a good time to evaluate other governance issues that may affect your safety culture.

Incident Response Team

The IRT should continue to concentrate on the areas related to responding to violations of policy:

1.   Develop document retention policies (Chapter 10)

2. Develop and schedule mandated reporter training for workers, parents, and other stakeholders (Chapter 10)

3. Start communicating mandated reporter policies to stakeholders (Chapter 10)

Child Safety Team

Likewise, the CST should continue the work that it has already started in the evaluation and drafting phases.

1. Now that you have defined your screening policies, audit the records for all your current employees and volunteers. Conduct whatever rescreening is necessary to meet your new standards.

2. Develop policies and standards for the following areas:
    - Use of pictures and videos of children (Chapter 6)
    - Offsite activities, if needed (Chapter 6)
    - Parent orientation on child safety policies (Chapter 9)
    - Training for children and youth, if you decide to have such training (Chapter 9)

3. Develop and schedule training for employees and volunteers in new child safety policies (Chapter 9).

4. Begin communicating child safety policies to stakeholders (Chapter 9).

5. Develop or find specialized training for people screening employees and volunteers (Chapter 5).

6. Consider needed upgrades in your physical facility (Chapter 7), develop a budget, and decide on a realistic timeline for potential changes.

Yearly Audits and Training

After you have your plan in place, you must establish the part that is the hardest for most organizations to do consistently. Making the child protection policy a part of your culture requires you to audit the policy frequently to be sure that it's still working for your organization. If it's not working, then you will need to either change your policy or increase your training and enforcement. But you must first identify the weaknesses in your child protection culture.

Once you know what changes you need to make, you can plan training for your staff. We recommend at least yearly training on child protection policies and mandated reporter responsibilities. People with specific responsibilities, such as those who are screening workers or part of the IRT, may need periodic training in those responsibilities as well.

Frequent Audits

We recommend audits at least yearly (more frequently if feasible) in the following areas:

Worker Documentation. At least once a year, have CST members go through the files of every adult who works with your program, including volunteers. Be certain that each file has the criminal records checks and reference checks that you have decided to require. If you are missing any criminal records checks, either remove the worker from contact with children or start supervising them, whichever route your jurisdiction requires or recommends, while you complete the missing checks.

If you are missing a large number of background checks, then you need to figure out why. Perhaps you are trying to do too many reference checks, or you need to assign more people to the task. CRCs are not optional, so figure out what you need to do to have a CRC for every adult in your program who might have unsupervised or regular access to minors.

Employee Assessments. A yearly audit is a good time to survey your staff, volunteers, and interns in several areas. First, have the CST give workers the Psychological Safety and Positive Accountability assessments again and compare the results from year to year. If the scores go down or plateau at a low level, then you have some culture issues that you need to address.

Along with the assessments, consider quizzing your staff and volunteers about your child protection policies. The CST can either distribute written questions along with the employee assessments or have informal lunch-and-learn discussions. In either instance, don't just ask workers to recite the rules. Use hypotheticals to learn if they know how to apply the rules in particular situations. Pull stories from the news or the industry grapevine to create hypotheticals and ask your staff in as low-pressure a manner as possible to tell you how they would handle each scenario. What you learn from these exercises will tell you what sort of training you need to do each year.

Incident Reports. Have both of your teams review all your discipline and incident reports from the prior year. Ask the CST to look for patterns or common weaknesses. For example, are your bullying incidents happening in a particular area in the school? Perhaps you need to assign more adult supervision to those areas. Even accidents can signal a looming safety problem that you need to address. Review as many records as possible to ensure that you have a comprehensive view of what's going on with child safety in your program.

Ask the IRT to view all the reports to assess the organization's response, and perhaps to conduct some tabletop exercises. Evaluate whether the organization has clear lines of responsibility and whether it has the right people performing those tasks. The IRT should focus on weaknesses in the response and the best ways to address those vulnerabilities.

Training

As we explain in later chapters, we recommend refresher training on your child protection and incident response policies at least yearly. It's a good idea to do this training after the yearly audits so that you know how to target the training. Yearly training is a good opportunity to do the tabletop exercises that we recommend later in this book. These exercises can build your organization's "muscle memory" without having to go through an actual incident.

We recommend, if possible, more frequent training in smaller chunks. Many of our clients include a safety reminder in routine weekly emails. Others designate a particular day for those emails, such as "Safety Monday." Lunch-and-learn sessions are a good way to focus on a particular topic or do some short tabletop exercises. In addition to attendance records, keep notes about feedback from these sessions so that you can use them in your yearly evaluation.

This chapter has been a quick overview of the process of creating a solid and workable child protection policy for your organization. The timetable above is a recommendation and, as always, you need to adjust it to your organization and its unique needs. By breaking the process down into manageable tasks, you will be able to develop your policy without getting overwhelmed. In the following chapters, let's get into the details for each of those tasks.

WORKSHEET #1

First 30 Days

Date Completed	Coordinator and Teams
	Name a Child Safety Coordinator (CSC)
	Knowledgeable, willing to become expert
	Has time and interest in staying up to date
	Ensures implementation of CPP
	Ensures reporting protocol
	Has authority to make policy & procedure changes
	Usually leads Incident Response Team
	Organization has committed to giving the CSC resources, time, and support
	Name a Child Safety Team (CST)
	Representative from stakeholder groups
	Board
	Administration
	Staff
	Parents
	Clients or Alumni
	Donors
	Other groups
	Experts in child protection

	People with authority to change policies and procedures
	Name an Incident Response Team (IRT)
	CSC
	Attorney
	Insurance expert
	PR expert
	Client/Parent contact
	Accused contact
	Employee contact
	Law enforcement/agency contact
	Information Manager
Date Completed	**Governance**
	Be sure your governing documents communicate how your student protection policy is grounded in the organization's mission and culture
	Have your governing documents reflect a commitment to child safety
Date Completed	**Initial Audit (*see Audit Worksheet*)**
	Complete initial audit

WORKSHEET #2

Student Protection Policy Initial Audit

Completed?		Standard of Care (Chapter 2)
		Assign CST to research standards of care in the field
		Applicable statutes, regulations, and licensing rules
		Standards that similar organizations follow
		Accreditation standards
		Association standards
		Local customs of similar organizations
Completed		Staff Surveys (Chapter 3 and Worksheet #3 and #4)
		Have staff and volunteers complete the Psychological Safety Survey
		Have staff and volunteers complete the Positive Accountability Survey
		Collate the results
		Note problem areas that need to be addressed by policies or training
Yes	No	Insurance (Chapter 10)
		Insurance covers child maltreatment, including sexual abuse
		Insurance covers potential defamation and emotional distress claims arising from mandated reports

		IRT has located all copies of old insurance policies
		Does the document retention policy require maintaining permanent records of insurance policies?
Yes	**No**	**Screening (Chapter 5 and Worksheets #8–10)**
		Do you screen all paid staff, volunteers, and interns who encounter minors?
		Does that screening include criminal reference checks, personal references, and individual interviews of the applicant?
		Do you have protocols for what checks to do for other adults in your program?
		Have you researched the best company to provide background checks for applicants?
		Do you have a policy regarding which negative background results will disqualify workers?
		Do you have a policy of documenting how you respond to negative background results?
		If you cannot screen all adults who may come in contact with students (e.g., during competitions open to the public), do you have supervision policies in place to protect students?
		Have you decided whether to have a waiting or supervision period for volunteers and clear guidelines for any exceptions?

Yes	No	Employment/Volunteer Application (Chapter 5)
		Does your application include permission for criminal records checks and questions to references?
		Does your application ask applicants about their criminal history and prior allegations of child maltreatment or boundary violations?
		Does your application require applicants to acknowledge by a signature that they understand the importance of your school's student protection policy?
		Does your application require applicants to acknowledge by a signature that providing materially false or incomplete information can be grounds for termination?
		Does your application require applicants to acknowledge by signature that violating your organization's mandated reporter policy can be grounds for discipline, including termination?
		Do you have a way of verifying the applicant's identity?
		How do you verify work and volunteer history?
		How many work reference checks do you conduct for each applicant?
		How many character reference checks do you conduct for each applicant?

Yes	No	
		Are those numbers for work and personal reference checks consistent with the standard of care in your industry?
		Do you have standard questions for all reference checks?
		Do you require an in-person interview for all staff, volunteers, and interns?
		Do you have a consistent policy regarding which volunteers do not need in-person interviews?
		Do you have standard questions for all in-person interviews?
		Do you have standard questions for work and personal reference checks?
		Do you have a policy of documenting all interviews and decisions about those interviews?
Yes	**No**	**Access Control (Chapter 6)**
		Do you have visitor access policies that limit access to minors on your campus?
		Do you have procedures to ensure that children are released only to parents/guardians with custody rights and their designees?
		Do you have procedures for refusing to release children when the receiving adult is intoxicated, under the influence, or otherwise poses a danger?

Yes	No	
		Do you have procedures for checking or supervising repair technicians, enhanced service providers, observers, and other visitors with business on your campus?
		Do you have procedures for supervising children at events open to the public?
		Have you clearly communicated to parents your expectations and guidelines for supervision at events open to the public?
		Have you investigated safeguards for active shooter situations?
Yes	**No**	**Behavior and Boundary Guidelines (Chapter 7)**
		Do you have an established worker to child ratio or specific supervision zones?
		Do you have procedures for monitoring and enforcing those ratios and zones?
		Do you have procedures for consistent monitoring of secluded areas, such as bathrooms or locker rooms?
		Do you know the problem areas for supervision and a policy for addressing those areas?
		If you have cameras, do you have policies that cover
		Retention time?
		Compensating for blind spots?
		Periodic review?

		Whether parents can view the video and any limits?
		Do you have clear restroom and hygiene policies for younger children?
		Can you realistically and consistently prohibit 1:1 interactions between adults and children?
		If so, do you have enforceable rules prohibiting those interactions?
		If not, do you have supervision and line of sight rules that provide sufficient protection for minors?
		Do you encourage positive interactions between individuals?
		Do you have clear guidelines about acceptable behavior boundaries between students and between students and adults?
		Do you have clear rules about on-campus use of technology?
		Do you have clear rules about acceptable contact between adults and minors off-campus or via social media and email?
		Have you communicated those rules to parents?
		Do you have clear rules about home contact, such as tutoring or babysitting?
		Have you communicated those rules to parents?

		If you allow off-campus contact, do you require waivers from parents?
		Have you developed rules that distinguish between positive mentoring and dangerous grooming?
		Have you communicated those rules to staff, volunteers, parents, and students?
		Do you have clear rules about what constitutes bullying?
		Do you have clear consequences for violation of rules about behavior and boundaries?
Yes	**No**	**Field Trips and Special Events (Chapter 6)**
		Do you have clear rules for field trips and overnight trips, including supervision, adult-to-child ratios, and transportation?
		If you cannot prohibit 1:1 adult-to-child contact, do you have adequate supervision (such as parents transporting their own child or caravans of private cars)?
		Do you require parental notifications and releases?
		Do you have clear supervision policies for events open to the public?
		Do you have clear and enforceable policies for use of pictures and videos of minors?

Yes	No	Mandated Reporter Policies and Training (Chapter 9)
		Has the IRT researched the requirements in your state?
		Do you have clear definitions of what must be reported?
		Do you have a clear procedure for reporting?
		Do you have a summary of the policies in the staff handbook?
		Do you have a summary of the policies in the parent handbook?
		Do you have staff training that meets the standard of care?
		Does your training cover likely scenarios for the age group that you serve?
Yes	**No**	**Staff & Volunteer Training (Chapter 9)**
		Does your staff sign a document agreeing to follow child protection policies?
		Do you train your staff shortly after hire on:
		Protection policies?
		Signs of abuse?
		Mandated reporter responsibilities?
		Behavior and boundary limits?
		Off-campus communications?
		Off-campus contact?
		Do you train your staff at least annually on the above topics?

		Do you have frequent, shorter trainings through the year?
		Do you document all of the training?
		Do you require training for volunteers on mandated reporting obligations?
		Do you document that training, whether through a vendor or in-house?
Yes	**No**	**Child and Parent Training (Chapter 9)**
		Have you considered age-appropriate training for minors?
		Have you notified parents about your child protection policies?
		Do you offer training to parents about your policies on boundaries and signs of abuse?
Yes	**No**	**Responding to Violations (Chapter 9 and Worksheets #13–14)**
		Do you have clear procedures for reporting violations of policy or concerns about whether someone has violated policy?
		Do your procedures include an avenue for reporting every position within the organization, from client to Board member or owner?
		Do you have protections for people who make reports of possible violations?
		Do you have clear procedures for responding to reports of inappropriate behavior?

		Do the members of the IRT have clearly-defined responsibilities for response?
		Do the members of the IRT know those responsibilities?
		Do your procedures set rules for responding to media inquiries?
		Have you communicated those rules to staff and volunteers?
		Does your IRT regularly conduct tabletop exercises to plan for appropriate response?
		Do you have clear criteria for determining when to institute an internal or external investigation?
		Do you have a plan for conducting an internal investigation?
Yes	**No**	**Physical Facility (Chapter 7)**
		Does your physical facility ensure clear sight lines for supervision of students?
		Do you control access to your facility and have a procedure for monitoring outside people while they are on the premises?
		Do you need to consult a safety coordinator to protect against active shooters?

Yes	No	Document Retention (Chapter 10)
		Do you have policies for retention of employee records?
		Do you have policies for retention of minor files?
		Do you have policies for retention of incident reports?
Yes	**No**	**Yearly Audits**
		Do you review your child protection policies at least annually?
		Do you audit your employee & volunteer files for background checks, references, and training at least annually?

WORKSHEET #3

Staff Assessment: Psychological Safety

For the following questions, please indicate your level of agreement or disagreement with the following statements using the following scale:

1: Strongly Disagree; 2: Disagree; 3: Neither Agree nor Disagree; 4: Agree; 5: Strongly Agree. For some questions, you can also choose NA ("not applicable").

1. I feel safe in reporting concerns that I have to my supervisor.

1	2	3	4	5

2. I know how to communicate to my supervisor any concerns about our policies and practices regarding abuse and injury prevention.

1	2	3	4	5

3. When I communicate my concerns to my supervisor, he or she listens.

1	2	3	4	5

4. When I communicate my concerns to my supervisor, he or she takes appropriate action.

1	2	3	4	5

5. I have reported concerns in the past and have felt my concerns were addressed.

NA	1	2	3	4	5

6. Our organization's leaders listen to front-line staff and seek their input and feedback.

1	2	3	4	5

7. I would feel comfortable reporting to leadership if I saw my supervisor violating policy or otherwise doing something I thought was wrong.

1	2	3	4	5

8. I would feel comfortable reporting to leadership if I saw another employee or a volunteer violating policy or doing something wrong.

1	2	3	4	5

9. The leadership of this organization truly values and supports its front-line staff.

1	2	3	4	5

10. I trust the people I work with.

1	2	3	4	5

WORKSHEET #4

Staff Assessment: Positive Accountability

1: Strongly Disagree; 2: Disagree; 3: Neither Agree nor Disagree; 4: Agree; 5: Strongly Agree. For some questions, you can also choose NA ("not applicable").

1. Protecting our beneficiaries and staff from abuse, neglect, and harm is a significant priority for this organization.

1	2	3	4	5

2. Our leaders give us regular feedback and training on how we can better protect our staff and the individuals we serve.

1	2	3	4	5

3. If I make a mistake at work, my supervisors are supportive and help me improve.

1	2	3	4	5

4. Our leaders are constantly looking for ways to improve the way we protect our staff and those we serve.

1	2	3	4	5

5. I have the tools and training I need to protect my fellow employees and those we serve from abuse and harm.

1	2	3	4	5

6. The rules we have at work for protecting staff and those we serve from abuse and injury are reasonable and easily implemented.

1	2	3	4	5

7. I feel empowered to use my best judgment in addressing problems at work.

1	2	3	4	5

8. Our staff members are highly motivated to protect each other and those we serve.

1	2	3	4	5

9. I frequently receive feedback and training from my leaders on issues of preventing abuse and harm to those we serve.

1	2	3	4	5

10. At my organization, we regularly discuss how to improve our protection of those we serve.

1	2	3	4	5

WORKSHEET #5

First 60–90 Days

Date Completed	Employee Files (CST)
	Audit employee files for criminal records checks
	Conduct checks on any employees missing them
Date Completed	**Insurance (IRT)**
	If needed, start locating insurance that covers abuse claims and defamation claims
	Continue to search for past insurance policies
Date Completed	**CST Develops Workable Policies**
	Use Feasibility Analysis (Worksheet #6) to evaluate proposed policies
	Identify current policies that are not working or are not being followed, and determine whether you:
	Need new/different policies, or
	Need better training or supervision
	Access Control Policies (Chapter 6)
	Screening Policies (Chapter 6)
	Application Policies (Chapter 5)
	Decide on probation period? (Chapter 5)
	Interaction Rules (Chapter 7)
	1:1 Contact or Supervision?
	Ways to work around limitations of physical facility

	Positive and clear rules about acceptable interactions between adults and children
	Positive and clear rules about acceptable interactions between children
	Positive and clear rules about contact between adults and children outside the organization (including waivers as needed)
	Rules that prohibit grooming behavior while not discouraging healthy mentoring
	Clear consequences for violation of rules
	Clear communication to parents, staff, volunteers, and children about rules and consequences
	Monitoring and Supervision Rules (Chapter 7)
	Staff:client ratios
	Zone supervision needed?
	Rules that protect minor volunteers, staff, and interns
	If organization has cameras, procedures for
	Retention
	Compensating for blind spots
	Periodic review
	Parent review
	Programs open to the public
	Child safety and supervision rules
	Policies for people with known criminal history or history of child maltreatment
	Clear communication to parents about policies and their responsibilities

Date Completed	IRT Develops Policies
	Whistleblower protections (Chapter 9)
	Receiving and responding to reports (Chapter 9)
	Mandated reporter standards (Chapter 10)
	Locate vendor or develop training on mandated reporter standards (Chapter 10)
	Written incident response plan
	Communications guidelines for all employees and volunteers

WORKSHEET #6

Feasibility of Implementation: Assessment

Think about a current child protection policy you have or perhaps a policy you are considering and respond to the following questions. The higher your score on this assessment, the more likely it is that the particular policy you are considering will have a positive impact.

1: Strongly Disagree; 2: Disagree; 3: Neither Agree nor Disagree; 4: Agree; 5: Strongly Agree.

1. This policy is well known and understood in our organization. (Or, if it's a proposed policy, leadership has already discussed it with staff and volunteers).

1	2	3	4	5

2. This policy is one that all the staff and volunteers agree is very important to child safety.

1	2	3	4	5

3. This policy is sufficiently clear, such that staff know when they've crossed the line.

1	2	3	4	5

4. It is hard for a person to violate this policy without others knowing about the violation.

1	2	3	4	5

5. If an employee or volunteer violates this policy, but no one says anything, harm to a child will likely occur.

1	2	3	4	5

6. This policy would be hard to violate, even for a "good reason."

1	2	3	4	5

7. There are few systemic issues in our organization that could create a situation in which a person might violate this policy.

1	2	3	4	5

8. No person with genuinely good intentions would ever consider violating this policy.

1	2	3	4	5

9. Following this policy is easy to do in our work environment.

1	2	3	4	5

10. Implementing this policy is fairly natural for our staff and organization.

1	2	3	4	5

WORKSHEET #7

First 120 Days

Date Completed	Employee, Volunteer, Intern Files (CST)
	Audit all worker files for criminal records checks
	Audit all worker files for reference checks per new policies
	Conduct checks on any employees missing them
Date Completed	**Board Governance**
	Encourage your Board to audit itself for good governance policies
Date Completed	**CST Develops Workable Policies**
	Document Retention
	Use of pictures and videos of children
	Parent orientation on child protection policies
	Offsite activities
Date Completed	**Training**
	CSC and CST develop and present training in new policies for all workers
	CSC and IRT develop and present mandated reporter training
	Consider training for children on safe boundaries
	CSC and CST develop and provide specialized training for those who screen employees and volunteers
	Consider needed upgrades to physical facility, develop realistic budget and timeline for potential changes

Yearly and Ongoing

Date Completed	Tasks
	Audit employee files for CRCs and reference checks
	Evaluate whether child protection policies are working
	Employee surveys
	Incident reports
	Training in child protection policies
	Training in mandated reporter policies
	Tabletop exercises (if possible)

CHAPTER 4

FINDING THE RIGHT LEADER AND TEAMS

"Fine," the camp director said. "We need to revamp our child protection policy, and I need to concentrate on fundraising and keeping the camp in business. So, I'll tell my assistant director to write a new policy for us. She already deals with these issues and she's good at fitting things into her to-do list."

EXPECTING ONLY ONE person to handle your child protection policy will set your organization up for failure. No single person can do everything involved in putting together a good child protection policy. This project requires a strong team of people. Actually, we recommend two strong teams with distinct responsibilities and skill sets—your child safety and incident response teams—and one strong leader for both. These teams will be the foundation of your child protection culture, so it is essential that you get the right people for these tasks. Be certain that they are knowledgeable (or willing to learn) and committed to creating a robust child safety culture in your organization.

CHILD SAFETY COORDINATOR

Every project requires a leader. Solid child safety policies require someone in charge of both creating them and ensuring that the organization follows them. Your first step, then, is to designate a Child Safety Coordinator (CSC). The CSC will be the key person in making the policy a part of your culture.

Be sure that your organization gives the CSC sufficient time and resources to do this job well. Too many times, we have seen clients simply add this role to the responsibilities of an assistant director or human resources manager. Those people certainly can be good CSCs, but not if they already have a full workload. Be ready to reassign projects so that the CSC can concentrate on the important—and ongoing—task of child protection.

Next, the CSC needs to be someone who is, or can become, knowledgeable about the field of child safety. Knowing the field is not something that the leader can delegate to one of the teams. The CSC will be the person to set the goals and strategy for the two teams, and therefore needs to thoroughly understand child protection principles.

The CSC also needs to be a person with leadership skills. Delegating tasks to a team doesn't automatically get the jobs done. The CSC will have to set measurable goals, deadlines, and opportunities for feedback. It will be the CSC's job to move the team along the timelines to complete this project.

Finally, the CSC needs to be someone with authority in the organization. As we discussed in earlier chapters, having written procedures is only part of a good child protection policy. The CSC needs to be someone who can both implement the procedures and hold people accountable. Some of our clients have named existing administrators as CSCs, while others have created a new position. Either strategy will work, as long as the CSC can make changes happen within the organization.

CHILD SAFETY TEAM

The first team we recommend is the Child Safety Team. This group will be responsible for evaluating, writing, and following up on the bulk of your improved child protection policy. While most of this team's work will be in the first 30–120 days of evaluating and creating or tweaking policies, this group also needs to continually evaluate how the organization is carrying out its responsibility of protecting children. So, choose members who are willing to make an ongoing commitment to the project.

Select team members who are willing to both learn and keep up with principles of child protection in your field. The CSC needs to be the main expert, but this is an area where many perspectives can help. Also, standards in the field can change, so you need as many people as possible to help keep up with new strategies. You may want to consult with an outside expert in child protection who can offer advice about new developments in your industry.

Furthermore, try to have a representative on your CST from each of your stakeholder groups. Many organizations treat child protection as though it's purely a human resources matter, but it's much broader. It's an organization-wide function. While it's inevitable that your employees will do most of the work, you need to hear from people throughout your organization. So, try to have at least one representative from each stakeholder group, such as a Board member, administrator (other than the CSC), staff, volunteers, and parents. If you have a current client who shows leadership, or a former client who has stayed involved, then definitely tap into that perspective. A person who is an expert on child protection policies or has the coordinator role at another organization also can provide helpful ideas.

Borrow a technique from the computer security world, where companies hire "ethical hackers" to probe for vulnerabilities in their systems. Have someone on your team think like a bad guy. That person's perspective can help the team identify holes in your organization's policies that you may not be aware of. Having the equivalent of an "ethical hacker" test your defenses can be an invaluable contribution to your policy.

Of course, you must include only people you can trust to have the organization's best interests at heart and to keep the team's work confidential. Evaluating a child protection policy will require a close look at the organization's internal workings, likely including some confidential information. To preserve confidentiality, you may need to limit some team members' access to information. Or you may want to create an auxiliary group, similar to a non-voting Advisory Board, to simply offer perspectives and information. Your needs will depend on your organization's mission and purpose. Your goal, however, is to have as many people as possible sharing the responsibilities consistent with confidentiality and good governance.

Be careful that you don't let one perspective control the direction of your policies. We have had clients rely too heavily on law enforcement or consultants or even attorneys, with the result that they missed some issues that other people with different skillsets could have warned them about. For example, they might have a policy that effectively keeps pedophiles out of the organization but doesn't address bullying very well. Child protection is one area where you need as many perspectives as possible to help you keep up with potential trouble spots.

Finally, be sure that the CST has enough members with authority that it can change policy. Having a paper-only policy is counterproductive—if you take away nothing else from this book, let it be this. Your team needs to be able to implement its recommendations and make child protection part of your organization's culture.

INCIDENT RESPONSE TEAM

The second team we recommend is the Incident Response Team, which every organization needs to have in place to respond to serious violations of policy and injuries. Most people assume that the IRT needs to be involved only after a serious incident. We recommend that this team start its work much earlier, from the beginning of the process, both to help avoid policy violations and to be better prepared if and when incidents happen.

We recommend that the IRT starts by evaluating and developing policies related to responding to incidents. For example, we have the IRT take responsibility for mandated reporting training, as that reporting is an integral part of any response to potential abuse. This training can also help prevent maltreatment by clarifying and reminding staff, students, and parents what behavior is off-limits.

Another purpose of the IRT is to help staff members prepare for a crisis. People who have never dealt with an incident before usually feel completely overwhelmed. They often react instinctively and make mistakes. If your IRT develops a process before you need it and ensures that everyone is trained, your staff is more likely to react calmly and appropriately if an incident does occur.

Some of our clients have a high overlap between the teams, with people taking roles on both teams. The CSC, for example, usually is the executive manager of the incident response team. How your organization should staff the IRT depends on your specific structure and needs, but we recommend that you consider people for the tasks listed below. Small organizations may need to have one person take on more than one task but be sure you spread the responsibility evenly enough to keep one person from becoming overwhelmed.

Fortunately, not every incident requires a full-court press. For a common athletic injury, for example, you likely will not need any public relations assistance. Nevertheless, be sure you have people available if needed for each the following tasks. It will be easier to recruit and not call them for common injuries than to scramble to find someone to help with a serious claim.

Executive Manager

This person is the main leader, responsible for knowing what everyone else on the team is supposed to be doing and is actually doing. If this leader is not the CSC for your organization, he or she needs to work closely with the CSC.

Attorney

This role can be filled by someone inside or outside your organization. If you are involved in litigation, your insurance will assign defense counsel to handle the lawsuit. Of course, you need to work with that attorney, but you also need separate counsel for several reasons.

First, we hope that you are putting together an IRT before you have any litigation. You need an attorney to review policies as early as possible and you may need help responding to an incident long before you have access to an insurance defense attorney. Waiting until you have an incident to get help for the IRT will be too late.

Second, an insurance defense counsel's primary responsibility and skill set are in resolving the lawsuit. He or she may not know enough about other areas to give you all the advice you need. These attorneys may not know anything about mandated reporting or whistleblower laws or public relations statements—all of which are very important areas for the IRT.

For the same reasons, you may not be able to rely on your organization's corporate counsel. Be certain that the attorneys you consult either know or are willing to learn the answers to questions unique to child protection policies.

Insurance Expert

The IRT will be responsible for (a) finding old insurance policies and (b) evaluating current insurance to be sure it covers all the organization's risks. Be sure the IRT has access to someone with the expertise to help with these projects.

Public Relations

If you have an incident, it's likely to hit social media at the speed of light. You need someone, either inside or outside your organization, to help with written statements and responses to both traditional and new media. Note that this person should *not* be a lawyer—very few lawyers have the skill set to write a good public statement. You will need to get your attorney's approval, particularly if there is a risk of litigation, but the initial author must be someone who understands public relations.

Client/Parent Contact

If you have an incident, you will need someone to be the contact point for the victim, other clients, and all the parents. In organizations with counselors on staff, it's common to use a counselor as the contact person. This works, as long as the counselor and the parents understand that the counselor is acting as an agent of the organization, not setting up a therapeutic relationship. As long as there is no confusion about roles, an empathetic counselor or other staff person can be a great choice.

This contact person needs to be someone who can walk a fine line between discretion and transparency. You cannot share all the details of your internal investigation, for example, but you need to answer the clients' and parents' legitimate questions. They will want to know, for example, if any minors are still at risk and what you are doing to protect the children in your care going forward. Your lawyer might not allow you to tell them what loopholes a perpetrator found in the organization, but you do need to be as transparent as possible about what care their children will receive going forward.

Employee/Accused Contact

You will need someone to be the contact person for the accused perpetrator, whether that's an employee or another minor. That representative needs to understand the need to treat everyone with respect and empathy during whatever investigation the organization is doing.

This respect is particularly important, because the first step in dealing with a claim (as we set out in Chapter 10) is suspending the accused. Whether the claim involves an employee or another student, someone will need to explain that the organization is not jumping to conclusions, but simply following protocol. Likewise, if internal investigators or law enforcement need to talk to the accused, then there needs to be a single contact person to facilitate those conversations.

You also need someone to be the contact person for your staff and volunteers. The last thing you need for morale is for workers to find out about the accusation via media reports. Your representative will need to exercise discretion in what facts they share, but you need to be as transparent with your employees as you are with parents and clients. This contact person also will be the person to remind employees about not sharing information outside the organization and where they can refer media inquiries.

The main responsibility of this contact person is to let employees know that the organization is paying attention to them and cares about them as well as everyone else in the middle of a crisis.

Law Enforcement/Agency Contact

If the incident is the subject of an official investigation, you need someone to be the point of contact with the investigators. Some regulatory agencies investigate as a matter of course, and administrators are well-versed in dealing with them. Law enforcement, however, can be much more intimidating. You need someone with experience either in being or dealing with law enforcement who can walk you through responding to their requests.

Law enforcement officers often come with a single priority, which is to investigate their case. They usually don't understand or are not concerned about your program, and likely do not understand the rules that you operate under. We often have cases where law enforcement demands records that regulatory agencies say are confidential, and we must explain those rules. You may need an attorney or other experienced person to help you navigate cooperating with law enforcement without compromising your overall mission.

Information Manager

Finally, you need someone to keep track of all the records involved, who is doing what, which agencies were contacted when, and all remaining tasks. This person also needs to be able to find all the internal records that you will need and keep track of what records you provided to which agency on which date. It is better for the IRT to have one person responsible for sending and keeping track of this information than for each individual team member to try to keep those records.

The CSC and these two teams will form the core of your child protection working group. You likely will not need everyone all of the time, and team members almost certainly will rotate in and out. Having as broad and strong a group as you can, however, will make it much easier for you to develop a strong child protection policy and make it a living part of your organization.

CHAPTER 5

SCREENING ADULTS WHO WORK WITH YOUR PROGRAM

"Yes, we screen all of our employees," said the school principal. "Well, we may be missing a reference check here or there, and I don't know how old the criminal records checks are, but I'm sure our records are in good enough shape. And we do interviews with everyone we can, although I don't like formal questions. I prefer to just talk and see where the conversation goes. We've never had any problems yet."

SCREENING ADULTS IS what most people think of when they talk about an organization's child protection policies, and it certainly is the first line of defense for your organization. Screening out potentially unsuitable workers is the best way to prevent future safety issues. Although no screening protocol is foolproof, there are ways to make your program stronger and to screen out the vast majority of predatory adults.

Screening employees involves questions of employment law that are complicated, unique to your local jurisdiction, and beyond the scope of this book. We set out general principles in this chapter, but we cannot predict how they apply to every jurisdiction or fact situation. You need to confirm and clarify all of these principles with a knowledgeable employment lawyer in your particular jurisdiction.

You do not always have to do the same level of screening for every adult who comes into your program. People doing maintenance or repairs, for example, need less screening than your full-time employees. Use the screening standards matrix in Worksheet #8 to help you decide which positions in your organization need which level of screening. The general dividing line is the level of consistent supervision that you can provide. For people who have sporadic contact with children and are always supervised, you do not have to stretch your budget to require extensive background checks. Similarly, when you cannot require background checks, such as for adults attending public events, you must closely supervise the minors in your care.

When developing your screening protocols, be alert to shifting responsibilities. A staff member may start out in a position that doesn't involve contact with children but later move to having more access. For example, you might hire a person as a cook who doesn't interact with children, but later you need him or her to temporarily supervise a classroom in an emergency. Similarly, a cook could transition to a teaching assistant. Determine your screening level based on the measure of access that a worker conceivably could have, and watch for transitions to jobs that need a higher level of screening.

If you opt for supervision in lieu of rigorous screening, then you must be sure that you are doing the supervision that you plan. As we discuss in Chapter 9 about implementing policies, it's all too easy to start cutting corners in the press of day-to-day deadlines. Getting too comfortable and lax about supervision of people without CRCs or clear reference checks is a weakness that predators can exploit. Failing in this area invariably will come back to haunt you.

APPLICATION

Your employment or volunteer applications can be a first line of defense against individuals who would present a risk to the children and youth you serve. By letting a potential staff member know that your organization takes child protection seriously and holds its staff and volunteers accountable for child safety, the application may itself act as a deterrent to predatory or risky adults. Therefore, in addition to your usual application questions and information, we recommend including several important features related to child protection.

Summarize your child protection mission on the application. This document is not the place to go into details about your child protection policy. But it is a good point to start emphasizing where child safety fits into your corporate culture. Include your mission statement or other short summary of the importance that your organization places on child safety concerns.

Include statements in which the applicant gives you permission to conduct a criminal records check (CRC) and to ask for information from work and personal references. Coordinate with your vendor for the language that you need for them to conduct a CRC and consult with an attorney or HR expert in your jurisdiction about the process and parameters for obtaining permission for CRCs and references.

Depending on the rules in your jurisdiction about the appropriate time in the process, ask the applicant about his or her criminal record, prior allegations of maltreatment, or prior concerns about boundary violations. This is a complex area of law with different rules depending on locality, so obtain legal advice before developing your list of questions. It is important not to ask about an applicant's criminal record at the wrong time or seek too much information, because violating local laws can expose you to discrimination claims. For example, your jurisdiction may prohibit you from asking about arrests that did not lead to conviction.

You may have to narrow the criminal record inquiry to crimes against children, but be as blunt as the law in your jurisdiction allows. If the law allows it, ask frankly if the applicant has ever been accused of mistreating or acting inappropriately toward a child. People who have mistreated children usually lie in response to these questions, but those lies give you grounds to terminate their employment later.

If an applicant reveals an accusation, then you will have to decide whether to continue with the application. It's possible that the accusation is one that doesn't deter you, such as a registry entry we once saw in which applicant was accused of "lack of supervision" for allowing her older child to walk alone to a nearby store. There also may be other factors (such as how long ago the conviction occurred or the applicant's age at the time) that the law in your locality requires you to consider. Whatever you decide, be certain that you clear your decision with your local attorney and document your decision and reasons for reaching it.

Require up front that the applicant, if hired, disclose any new arrest, change in professional licensing status, or new involvement with child protective services, to the extent that your locality allows the requirement. Explain in the application that failure to voluntarily disclose will be grounds for discipline. You need to include this provision in a staff handbook as well, but the application is a good place to start making this point.

Include a statement that giving any materially false or incomplete information on the application can be grounds for discipline or termination. This provision will allow you to deny or terminate employment if you discover a relevant criminal conviction or child maltreatment substantiation that the applicant didn't disclose.

Include a statement advising the applicant that failing to follow your internal procedure for making a mandated report can be grounds for discipline or termination. You need to establish from the beginning of the relationship that your organization takes its mandated reporting obligations seriously. It also is good to let people know early that you have a procedure that you expect them to follow so that your organization can provide help and follow up as needed.

Finally, get the applicant to sign a statement agreeing to all the provisions listed above that your locality allows. Your legal counsel will know what language your application needs for the signature to become part of the employment agreement. You must make child safety a part of your agreement with all your workers from the very beginning of each relationship.

BAN THE BOX

Some states have adopted a "ban the box" policy that prohibits use of criminal records for employment decisions. Even those states, however, generally have an exception for youth organizations, allowing them to screen employees and volunteers who will be working with children. Talk to a lawyer who is familiar with the rules in your jurisdiction about what CRCs the law allows for organizations like yours and when you can ask for the CRCs.

CRIMINAL RECORDS AND REGISTRY CHECKS

Your first line of defense against dangerous people will be criminal records checks (CRCs) for workers. CRCs are essential and included in every jurisdiction's standard of care. Frankly, it will be rare these days to have someone with a child maltreatment conviction apply for a job with youth organizations. Simply asking for a CRC usually will deter people with such a background. If you don't require a CRC, however, you are creating a dangerous hole in your child protection program that a predator can exploit. CRCs only work when everyone uses them.

The first question you must decide is which CRCs to do for which positions. Your choices are local checks or more extensive, and more expensive, national record checks. The FBI will allow many government licensing agencies to access its nationwide database. If your organization is subject to licensing, then you probably don't have any decisions to make. You simply follow your licensing rules.

If you do not have access to a government agency's resources, you must decide which records you want to search. As we outline in Worksheet #8, you don't need the same level of screening for every position. If your budget allows national checks for everyone, then, by all means, do the most thorough investigation you can. If your budget is limited, however, triage what you need. Always be certain that you do not pick and choose whom to ask for a CRC based on demographics or any factor other than access to children, as this sort of arbitrary decision easily leads to discrimination claims.

The reason that national checks are more expensive is that there is not a single outlet that you can check for applicants. The FBI, for example, will provide an individual's criminal background to that individual, but not to anyone else. While you could require an applicant to obtain that record and provide it to you, we have seen a number of applicants edit the official records to produce convincing fake clearances. The only way to be sure that you have an accurate CRC is to get it directly from each state's database or a vendor with access to those databases. The only practical way to get a nationwide check, then, usually is to go with a reputable vendor.

Some jurisdictions allow you to charge volunteers and even employees for the cost of a CRC. Check with an attorney who knows the laws in your state to determine if you can ease your budget by shifting these costs. That shift may make vendors' checks affordable enough for you to require nationwide checks for more positions.

Local CRCs involve asking a local sheriff's office or police department to run a check and provide you with the records. Most such agencies can run checks for the entire state. What you can learn about someone else's records may be limited. For example, you may only learn about felonies and not get a record of DUI convictions or misdemeanor drug possession. If those type of offenses matter, then you likely will be forced to work through a vendor that checks those records.

Finally, be sure that you or your vendor checks public sex offender registries. Every state has these registries online for anyone to search. It is true that the odds of one of your applicants being on your state's sex offender registry are low. The odds, however, are not zero, so you need to conduct that check for every applicant.

MALTREATMENT REGISTRIES

Almost every state has a registry of people against whom state agencies have substantiated some form of child maltreatment. These registries are not CRCs or sex offender registries, which capture criminal proceedings. Child maltreatment registries list people who, according to child protective services, have mistreated or neglected a child, whether or not they were prosecuted. These offenses are not criminal, and the burden of proof is lower than for criminal charges. Thus, the registries capture a much wider range of behavior.

Most state registries limit who can access the information. In many states, organizations that work with children can get the records for employment purposes. Check with your state child protection authorities to see if you can get the information and determine what releases you need from the applicant to access it. If you work with a vendor, be sure to discuss whether and to what extent that organization can access registry information.

DECIDE WHICH OFFENSES WILL DISQUALIFY WORKERS

Once you decide which CRCs to conduct for which positions, start thinking about which offenses will disqualify people for those positions. This probably will be an evolving list as you get CRC results, in part because you need to be sure that the CRCs are not creating a claim of disparate impacts on employee decisions, but you should start thinking through general principles as early as possible. For example, a DUI conviction may not matter for a cook in your school, but it would be disqualifying for a bus driver. Similarly, different organizations will have differing opinions about marijuana possession charges or underage drinking.

When you create guidelines for disqualifying convictions or determinations, make sure you include *why* certain offenses result in automatic disqualification and the factors to consider for offenses for which there is discretion to hire. Whatever your guidelines, put them in writing so that you can apply them consistently. Decide, for example, who reviews the file when a CRC comes back with a conviction. Some organizations leave the ultimate decision to the hiring manager, while others require another administrator or committee to weigh in.

Whoever does the review, keep information about CRCs confidential. Use the CRC results only for the purpose of determining eligibility for employment. Also be certain that there is a review for every applicant with a conviction or other negative record. Document whatever decision you make. If you decide not to hire the person because of the conviction, you will need a record to protect your organization in the case that the applicant reports you for unfair treatment. If you decide to hire the person or allow access as a volunteer, you may need to justify that decision to other parties later. Whether you think the offense is one that doesn't affect job performance, or was many years ago, or involves extenuating circumstances, put your reasons in writing and put that document into the file.

Do the same for any record from the child maltreatment registry. The registry may not give you any details of the substantiation, so you may have to decide whether you can trust the applicant's explanation. You will likely find that maltreatment registries, because of broad definitions and lower standards of proof, often reflect decisions by overly enthusiastic case workers. Thus, you may have more leeway in hiring people despite their placement on a registry. For example, some states are more prone than others to cite homeschooling parents for educational neglect. We have seen parents cited for lack of supervision for letting children play in nearby parks by themselves. Not every substantiation is equal, and you should review each one individually. You do not want to lose good people by a blanket disqualification, nor do you want to allow access to a person who has actually mistreated children in the past.

RINSE AND REPEAT

CRC and registry checks are not a one-time process. You need to recheck all your employees and volunteers every few years so that you catch any later offenses. How often to do the checks depends on the standard in your industry, but the most common time frames that we see are every five to eight years. We recommend that in your yearly audits, you note the dates of the last checks for each employee and when it will be time to do those checks again. Seek advice from your attorney about whether you will need to request consent again from employees to update their CRCs.

REFERENCE CHECKS

Your second line of defense is hearing from people who know the applicant better than you do. Checking past work references is standard, but we also recommend checking with personal references when you can. There are two very important reasons for asking applicants to list personal references.

First, personal references will have a different perspective than employers or coworkers. Friends usually see applicants in their less-guarded moments and in a different context than their workplaces. Personal references also can give you more relevant information about applicants without much work experience or coming from a different field. An office staffing agency, for example, can tell you whether your applicant showed up on time and worked hard, but no one there will be able to tell you how he or she interacted with children. Friends and volunteer youth organizations will be the people with that information.

A second, and perhaps more important, reason for contacting personal references is that they will usually give you more information. Many employers will only confirm dates of employment and tell you whether the applicant is eligible for rehire. Lawyers have taught employers to avoid defamation suits by limiting the information that they provide, so even if the applicant is not eligible for rehire, the employer typically won't tell you why. In rare instances, an employer might have agreed as part of a separation agreement not to provide any negative information to anyone who asks for a reference. In all these situations, you simply will not have access to the sort of information that you need to gauge whether the applicant poses a danger to children.

Personal references don't have such restrictions. Friends and acquaintances generally will speak more freely than past employers and give you much more information. Of course, in most situations, you will be hearing a friend's bias rather than an employer's more objective thoughts. But you might be surprised at how often you will hear less-than-stellar opinions, particularly if you explain that the job involves the care of children.

Whatever mix of personal and work references you decide on, we recommend several important principles for checking references:

Require two to five total reference checks. The exact number will depend on the standards in your field and how much manpower you can devote to the task. Be realistic about how many hours your staff can spend calling references. Get as much information as you can from as many sources as you can, but don't set a standard that interferes with the rest of your program.

Pay attention to gaps in an employment record. It's not unusual for people who had trouble at a job to simply leave it off their employment history. They often cover the gap by claiming to have taken time off for education or to spend time with family, but don't take the applicant's word for it. Get a transcript directly from the school and ask about personal references who can confirm the time off. This is one area where personal references may provide the information that you need. Friends and volunteers rarely know about false claims of taking time off, and they often will tell you what they know about that time in the applicant's life.

Use standardized questions when checking references. Using questions that you have worked out with your legal counsel or hiring expert helps you know, first of all, that the questions don't run afoul of anti-discrimination laws. Standardized questions also help you remember which areas you need to cover when doing reference checks. You don't have to use the same questions with all applicants. We've seen the best results from having a menu of questions that an interviewer can choose from, taking particular relevant facts into account. Consult with your legal counsel about possible discrimination claims from the appearance that you are scrutinizing one applicant more closely than others. Among the questions you ask, be sure to include several that will help you learn how an applicant tends to interact with children. We have included some suggested topics and reasons for the topics in Worksheet #10.

APPLICANT INTERVIEWS

The next important component of your child safety policy is an individual interview. You may not have the resources to interview every volunteer involved in your program. For example, programs that use parent chaperones for field trips rarely have time to conduct employment-style interviews with each parent. Just as with CRCs and reference checks, use Worksheet #8 to help you determine which positions need in-depth personal interviews.

As with reference checks, we recommend that you have a standardized set of questions to pull from when interviewing applicants. You don't have to use the exact same questions with every applicant, but you should give your hiring administrators a range of pre-established questions to choose from. Work with your legal counsel or hiring expert in your jurisdiction to develop language for the questions that meets the laws and regulations in your state and avoids the appearance of discrimination based on illegal factors.

Be sure that your list of questions includes questions related to an applicant's suitability for work with children. Worksheet #9 lists some topics for you to consider. Some of the topics, such as how an applicant spends his or her free time, would be problematic in interviews for most jobs because they could be a back-door way to inquire about prohibited areas, such as religion or ethnic origin. For youth organizations, however, they can be an important indicator of whether the applicant has an unhealthy interest in children. Be certain that your legal advisor understands how the questions relate to legitimate considerations (bona-fide occupational qualifications or BFOQs) for youth organizations and that he or she helps you frame the questions in a way that your jurisdiction allows.

Document all the questions that you ask and all of the responses. If you ever need to retrace the hiring process, either to defend your decision or make a disciplinary decision, you will need to know that information. Rough notes are fine, as long as they contain all the relevant information.

PROBATION PERIOD

Consider whether you can have a probation period for all new hires or volunteers. During this time, the worker would have limited autonomy and constant supervision. Some organizations opt for "working interviews" before bringing the applicant on board. In either situation, be certain that you allow access to children only *after* you have received a CRC report on the applicant.

Also be certain that your local laws and regulations allow probation periods and clear the practice with your legal counsel. Also consult with your attorney about whether you must pay employees during this probationary time or "working interview."

Probation periods allow you to have experienced employees observe an applicant's interactions and offer guidance. More importantly, it gives your experienced staff an opportunity to catch problematic behavior before a worker has unfettered access to children.

Not every organization has the resources to require a probation period. If your program can't afford to double staff during a probation period, try to have enhanced informal supervision at beginning of the worker's service. Ask your administrators to drop into the new worker's area as often as possible and train your experienced staff to check in with the new worker frequently. Not only will they be able to help the new person adjust to your program, but "supervising by walking around" can uncover a lot of problems before they become major issues.

DOCUMENTATION

You need to document everything that you can when screening applicants, but be especially sure that you have a written record of the following parts of screening.

Records Checks

Be sure that you document the CRC report, sex offender search, and inquiries to child maltreatment registries for each worker. Keep those records in the file as long as you keep the file, unless your locality requires you to destroy them earlier. Also, consult with your attorney about whether you must keep the information separate from other employee records. If you discover in your audits that you are missing any of these records, have the checks done again immediately so that you are able to document a clear record.

Interview

Document the questions that you asked in any interviews and the responses. Rough notes are fine as long as you make them as accurate and complete as possible. If you decide against an interview for a particular worker, you might want to note in the file the reason why you made that decision, such as "parent chaperone," or "always supervised."

References and Follow-up

Document all the work and personal references that you are able to contact. This may be the most common deficiency we see in clients' records. They intend to call references but lose track of the task in the bustle of other daily responsibilities. Keep a record not only of who you called, but how they responded to which questions. We recommend that you check this documentation in yearly audits of worker's files and backfill any references that you may be missing.

Exceptions

Always document your reasons for accepting someone who has anything negative on their record. The reason can be as simple as noting that the offense is a DUI and their duties will not include transporting children. Whatever the offense, document that you are aware of it, considered it, and made a reasoned decision about it.

Screening applicants to your program is an essential part of protecting the children in your care. Use your application, interview, CRCs, and reference checks to the fullest extent that your attorneys advise and your locality allows to avoid problematic behavior that could put young people at risk.

WORKSHEET #8

Screening Standards

Access to Children	Positions (Examples)	Screening Level	Screening Components
Frequent	Teachers, Staff, Bus Personnel	5	<ul><li>Verify identity</li><li>Work and volunteer history</li><li>State/ national CRCs</li><li>Sex offender registry</li><li>Child maltreatment registry</li><li>2–5 reference checks</li><li>Personal interview</li></ul>

Access to Children	Positions (Examples)	Screening Level	Screening Components
Sporadic	Volunteers	4	• Verify identity • Waiting period • State/national CRCs • Sex offender registry • Child maltreatment registry • At least 1 reference check • Personal interview
Sporadic with supervision	Lunchroom personnel, Outside vendors or repair contractors, Classroom speakers, Some volunteers, Board members, Parents	3	Local CRCs, registry checks, and interviews for employees and volunteers where you can require; otherwise ensure adequate supervision.

Access to Children	Positions (Examples)	Screening Level	Screening Components
Other Youth Organizations	Intramural competitions (judges, referees, other team coaches), Accreditation visits	2	No screening, BUT include in any agreement your expectations that organization has screened its personnel. Reinforce that expectation in writing (e.g., emails and keep copies)
Public	Public competitions and events	1	No screening, BUT ensure adequate supervision of potential and unexpected interactions with students/minors.

Principles to Remember

Don't plan it unless you can perform it. Be certain that you can consistently execute whatever policy you develop. The only thing worse than not having a policy is having one that you don't follow. If you are sued, not only will your written policy set the standard for what you should have done, but not following it will allow claims that you didn't follow any of your written policies.

Supervision ≈ screening. It's not always feasible to insist on background screening for adults who enter your organization, such as parents eating lunch with their child or special speakers or repair people. Always follow the rule that, when you can't screen, you insist on supervision by a fully screened employee.

Adapt screening rules for your organization. For some policies, the content doesn't matter as much as having a consistently enforceable (and enforced) policy. For example, you don't have to have a volunteer waiting period; you simply have to *decide* whether or not you will have one. If you decide you need one, you can have a shorter waiting period for volunteers who have a right to be involved (parents or guardians) than volunteers with no ties to your school. You also can have a tiered waiting period, such as limiting a parent's involvement to their child's group for a period of time or requiring supervision by another fully screened staff member or volunteer for a set time.

Screening Audit/Checklist

Name	Position	Screening Level	Screening Components Required for Level	Date Each Completed (if Exempt, Note Reason)	Service Start Date

WORKSHEET #9

Topics for Applicant Interview Questions

In addition to your standard questions about credentials and experience, we recommend that you develop questions about as many of the following topics as you can fit in. Phrase the questions to fit your organization's needs, and work with your attorney to stay within your jurisdiction's anti-discrimination laws. Be sure that your attorney is experienced in working with youth organizations, as most jurisdictions will allow YSOs more leeway than other employers to ask about matters such as volunteer and non-work activities. In the explanations below, we list some reasons that these topics are bona-fide occupational qualifications (BFOQs) for youth organizations.

Preference for age/sex of youth: If an applicant seems fixated on particular ages or genders, you need to ask more questions. The applicant may have a good reason, such as prior experience with or unique understanding of a particular age group. You need follow-up questions to rule out predatory intent.

What would others say about their ability to work with minors: How an applicant answers these sorts of questions may raise red flags about his or her prior experience.

Activities and hobbies: These questions will help you determine if applicants have healthy adult relationships. A lack of adult friendships should raise red flags for you.

Why the applicant wants the job: These sorts of questions may help you note immaturity or bad intent in seeking access to children.

How the applicant would handle specific scenarios: Pose hypothetical situations that test their understanding of boundaries and other interactions, as well as their willingness to correct boundary violations that they see. Avoid topics that the average lay person would not know, such as the intricacies of mandated reporter law in your state.

What abilities are most important for working with children or teens: This question helps you gauge whether the applicant understands your program. It also helps you gauge how the applicant views what is involved in interacting with minors.

Biggest weakness or strength when mentoring children or teens: Again, this question helps you understand the applicant's maturity and experience, as well as giving you the opportunity to probe for boundary violations.

Experience and skill in handling depressed, anxious, or lonely young people: This question explores an applicant's understanding of situations that are likely to arise in your program, as well as helping you determine whether the applicant understands boundary guidelines when helping vulnerable young people.

WORKSHEET #10

Topics for Reference Checks

In addition to your standard questions about credentials and experience, we recommend that you develop questions about as many of the following topics as you can fit in. Phrase the questions to fit your organization's needs, and work with your attorney to stay within your jurisdiction's anti-discrimination laws. The explanations below include some reasons that these topics are bona-fide occupational qualifications (BFOQs) for youth organizations.

How the applicant relates to young people: This question leaves room for the reference to note any problematic behavior that they might have observed.

How the applicant relates to adults: This question allows you learn whether the applicant has healthy and mature adult relationships, or only socializes with young people. The latter can be a red flag indicating that the applicant will not observe healthy boundaries.

Situations where the reference has observed the applicant interacting with youth: Questions asking for descriptions of those situations will allow you to determine whether the reference has the information that the applicant claims.

Whether the reference would be willing to place his or her child in the applicant's care: This question may reveal whether the reference really believes that the applicant is dependable and a positive influence on young people. If you sense any hesitation or waffling in the response, you need to ask more questions.

Whether the reference has any reason you should not consider the applicant for a position: It is surprising how many references, particularly personal references, are willing to provide less-than-flattering information in response to this question.

How the reference would rate the applicant's ability to follow policies and procedures: This question helps you understand whether the applicant will follow your child protection policies, as well as other internal expectations.

How the reference would rate the applicant's ability to maintain appropriate interpersonal boundaries: This is another question that often elicits surprisingly frank opinions.

CHAPTER 6

CONTROLLING OUTSIDE ACCESS TO YOUR PROGRAM

"We thoroughly screen every adult who comes into our program," said the camp director. "Well, at least our employees. I don't know about the plumber who made the emergency call last Friday night, or the accreditation counselors who visited earlier this week, and I don't even want to think about all the parents on drop-off and pick-up days. How can we possibly screen everyone who comes onto our property?"

SCREENING POLICIES WILL help you vet the people who work for and represent your organization. The next step is to consider the people whom you do not employ, but who visit your facility for various reasons. This group would include repair people, visitors, and those who provide specialized services, such as therapists or arts instructors.

For each of these people, you will have to decide two things. First, you must decide whether to conduct background checks. The matrix in Worksheet #8 gives you some guidelines on what sort of screening you might want to consider based on your ability to supervise the person's access to children. Then, you need to consider what sort of restrictions you can place on people whom you cannot screen.

The principles for deciding who has access to the children in your care will vary according to your organization's unique mission and physical facility. Schools, for example, usually have more ability to control physical access than outdoor camps. Similarly, groups that are open to public audiences, such as churches or sports leagues, will not be able to do background checks on every adult present and will have to rely instead on close supervision of minors. As with all the principles in this book, adapt the following principles about access control to the needs of your organization's mission and circumstances.

VISITORS

The first, and easiest, group of people you need to consider are outside visitors who don't have the legal rights of parents or guardians. Therapists and repair people, for example, are on your campus by invitation, and you can require screening or limit their access as you wish. Remember that some licensing and regulatory authorities may require a level of background checks or constant supervision for visitors to your facility. In general, for any visitors, we recommend that you consider the following principles:

Require everyone to check in and check out. You need a record of when and how long these visitors are on your campus and which areas they are visiting.

Require each person to confirm his or her identity. If a visitor comes regularly, such as an enhanced services provider, your staff will get to know them and will not need to check ID every time. But make sure that your staff checks ID the first time someone visits and whenever you have a new worker on duty who doesn't know them.

If you plan to supervise the visitor in lieu of screening, be consistent in your supervision. Just as with employees, it is all too easy to start liking and trusting a frequent visitor and then cut corners on a policy. If there is a chance that the person will have unsupervised access in the future, go ahead and follow your full screening protocol.

If you can't continually supervise or require screening, then limit physical access. If you have an involved repair project, for example, you may not have enough staff to assign someone to supervise the repair crew the entire time it is at your facility. You also rarely have time to wait for a criminal background check to come back if you have a pressing repair. In those cases, you need to physically separate the repair crew from your youth. Notify the staff that the area is off-limits and post signs to remind everyone. Even better, put up barriers that will physically separate the visitors from your program's activities.

MENTORS

Sometimes mentors will want to visit with mentees at your program. In past years, for example, it was common for religious leaders to have lunch at school with members of an organization's youth members. In other instances, tutors met with students during after-school programs or in the library during lunch. Minors also like to have their mentors attend family days at camp or games in sports leagues.

If your organization decides to allow outside mentors into your program, be sure you implement the following safeguards:

1. **Know the difference between healthy mentoring and predatory grooming behavior.** You can find some important distinctions in Chapter 7 of this book. Be aware of the interactions between the mentor and the minor so that you can notice any problematic behavior.

2. **Get written permission from parents.** One of the characteristics of predatory groomers is their tendency to emotionally isolate victims from their families and friends. Be certain that you keep parents in the loop about every mentor who visits with a child in your program.

3. **Ensure adequate supervision.** Never let a mentor and any youth visit in an isolated area. Restrict them to populated areas with clear sight lines, such as a dining hall or school library. There is never a healthy reason for a mentoring adult and youth to be out of sight of your staff.

PARENTS

Parents are in a different category from other visitors. It is always a good idea to encourage parent involvement in your program, both to strengthen your working relationship with parents and to benefit their children. Involved parents also help your child protection efforts by giving you additional people to watch over the youth. Youth can never have too many caring people watching out for them.

Even with all those benefits, you still need policies about parents' visiting youth at your facility or picking them up. Here are the major policies that you need to consider and adapt for your program:

Know who has the authority to pick up each child at the end of your program. If you are dealing with divorced or separated parents, be sure that you know who has custody rights. If you expect to have long-term involvement with the family, such as school, then get a copy of the custody order. If yours is a short-term program, such as a summer camp, put a statement in the agreement that the parent signs in which they certify that they have legal authority to enroll their child in the program and pick them up afterward. Be sure to have a way of identifying people that parents may send in their stead.

Have a procedure for releasing the child only to designated people. For younger children, you may need to have parents, or their designees, show ID to ensure that you are releasing the child to the correct person, at least until your staff is able to identify parents or relatives without the ID. If you have a lot of children leaving at the same time, having each parent park and come inside may not be practical. We have some clients who give parents a laminated car pass with an assigned number. Whomever the parents give the car pass to has the ability to pick up that child in the car lane at the end of the day. Whatever procedure works for your program, find a way to ensure that you are releasing a given child only to authorized people.

Have a policy and train your staff about what to do if they suspect that someone who is picking up a child poses a danger. We've seen cases where parents arrived under the influence of alcohol or marijuana, making it dangerous to release the child to them. The proper steps for handling such situations vary according to your state's laws but be sure that you have a policy for responding to those situations and that your staff knows and is empowered to enforce it.

Develop a policy about parents' visiting children while they are in your program. In most states, you can't completely restrict parents from educational programs, but you can limit their attendance. Other programs, such as camps, encourage children to be independent, and thus limit parents' ability to drop in and disrupt the schedule. Whatever rules work for your program, be certain that you have communicated them clearly to parents and that the parents have consented ahead of time.

If you cannot require screening, such as states where parents have a right to visit your program any time, then be sure that you have adequate supervision. You may not need to monitor parents' interactions with their own children, but you need to be able to observe any interactions with other children. And, just as with any visitor, avoid allowing adults to meet with children alone.

EVENTS WITH PUBLIC ACCESS

Many youth organizations have events that are essentially open to the public. Camps, for example, will have parents' visiting days, and it is simply not practical to screen all the adults present on those days. Youth sports leagues always have parents and relatives attending public games, and there is no practical way to know whether an adult has a legitimate reason to be there or is a predator checking out potential victims.

The only solution in those situations is to double down on the supervision of the minors in your care. Consider putting the following provisions into your policies:

Decide who will supervise which minors, how, and when. For example, who will supervise the team members during away games? Develop rules about who can travel with the team, where the team members will be when, and who is responsible for supervising them from door to door.

If the events are on your premises, be sure that you have enough staff to supervise known or potential problem areas. You may need to do spot checks of bathrooms, for example, or under the bleachers. Furthermore, remember to focus on risks other than abuse, including safety hazards. At camps, for example, you need to be sure that your swimming area still has someone checking it when you don't have any swimming events planned.

Be clear with parents about the limits of your ability to supervise the general student body in public situations. Have clear statements in your parent handbooks or event flyers that parents are responsible for supervising their own children during these public events.

VISITORS WITH CRIMINAL HISTORY

One question that sometimes comes up is what to do with visitors who have a known criminal history. For example, we have had youth sports leagues call us when a parent of team member showed up on a sex offender registry. The courts hadn't imposed any restrictions, and the leagues had no ability to exclude a parent from an event open to the public. In those situations, we recommend that you learn from organizations that have dealt with the issue for several decades, specifically houses of worship that have sex offenders attending services. You can find many good policies on the Internet, but you should consider all the following principles:

Limit the offender's involvement to public events. Make it clear that they cannot coach, mentor, transport, or otherwise interact with the minors in your program other than their own children.

Have them agree not to interact with any of your young people (other than their children) outside the program. For example, they will not host any slumber parties or otherwise allow children in your program to visit with their children in their home. The only exception to the no-contact rule would be if the other minors' parents signed a release after full disclosure of the criminal record. In one instance, we had a client camp learn of a parents' criminal record after all the parents in the cabin knew about it. It was a decades-old statutory rape conviction, and the other parents weren't concerned about it. You can't override such parental decisions. All you can do is notify the parents (in writing) and try to get a written release from them.

Get all these assurances in a written, signed agreement. Make it clear that the penalty for a violation is an immediate ban from your program.

Finally, decide when and how to notify other parents in your program. You may or may not see a risk that they need to know about. You don't want to breach privacy limits unnecessarily, but your first priority must be protecting the children in your care.

FIELD TRIPS AND PHOTOS

A final miscellaneous category is what sort of rules you need about field trips and taking photos or videos of minors. Those are very different situations, but they have a couple of overlapping principles.

Field Trips

If you transport minors off your campus, first be sure that you have clear rules about supervision. As at public events, know which adult will be supervising which minors and when. If constant supervision is not practical, such as on a trip to an amusement park for teenagers, then be sure that parents know about and have agreed to the unsupervised times.

Next, look at your transportation arrangements. Require every adult in a vehicle with minors to have a clear criminal background check. Decide how your rules about one-on-one contact will work in this situation and make any changes you need to be sure that the minors are protected. If you can, use a bus or van instead of a caravan of private cars. If you don't have the budget to provide a single mode of transportation, then be sure that you have solid background checks on adults who are driving and written permission from all the minors' parents. Even better, include a release in that permission form if your state allows it. Finally, be sure your liability insurance covers parents who volunteer to drive children other than their own.

Photos

Most youth programs want to show pictures of happy children in their advertising and social media pages. Be sure that you have written permission from parents to use their children's images in public displays. Be particularly careful if you serve special populations of minors to make sure that you are acting within regulations and parents' permission. Foster children, for example, usually may not be shown in any public manner. Even when you have parental consent, you must also consider whether publishing a photo of a child might improperly invade the child's privacy or be viewed as exploiting the child. This latter issue frequently arises for organizations that serve children and youth suffering adversity, so be sure your policies are clear.

We don't encourage you to be paranoid about allowing visitors to your organization or taking your kids to public events. Many programs have a mission of serving all comers, and many others want to be welcoming to as many people as possible. Field trips are an important way to broaden kids' horizons, and public events are unavoidable for many programs. You don't need to change your mission to have a strong child protection policy, but you do need to be realistic about the risks you face and take any measures you can to protect the children in your care.

CHAPTER 7

ESTABLISHING BEHAVIOR AND BOUNDARY PROTOCOLS

"Well, we have a long section in our staff handbook on codes of conduct," said the director. "But, I've had to let several staff go recently for rule violations, and now we're short-handed. I can't pay attention to all the picky rules again until we get fully staffed."

THE NEXT TASK is auditing, writing, or tweaking the behavior guidelines that you expect your staff and students to follow. Usually, this is the job of your Child Safety Team. As you go through the suggestions in this chapter, remember that your goal is a group of policies that you can follow consistently and impartially.

ADULT/YOUTH CODES OF CONDUCT

Codes of conduct for the adults in your program are a good place to start working on your child protection policies. Strong boundary guidelines are an important line of defense, allowing you to recognize problematic behavior before an adult becomes actively dangerous to children. As you work on your codes of conduct, keep the following principles in mind.

Use positive, specific language. The first principle we recommend is that you start with positive language in your staff and volunteer codes of conduct and continue using it whenever possible. If you start by encouraging positive interactions, it sets a much better tone for interactions than a list of "thou shalt nots." Using positive language also allows you to encourage people in a positive direction rather than frightening them into compliance.

In that positive language, emphasize the worker's role as an adult mentor rather than a friend. Many staff and volunteers, particularly young adults, have a hard time remembering that they are now the adults in the room and not peers. Programs that use junior staff, such as many summer camps, may find that they need to put a special emphasis on this role change.

Also, give specific examples of good behavior when you can. For example, do "acts of kindness" include sending birthday cards, or just praising students when they succeed? Not all these examples need to be in your official codes of conduct. You may want to highlight positive interactions between your adult workers and students in group emails or lunch-and-learn sessions during the year. Whenever you can find opportunities to give your workers specific examples, do it.

Use specific definitions in your codes of conduct. You need to use as specific language as you can when setting out your expectations for your staff. It's true that you may need to have broad language, such as "inappropriate contact," in a handbook. However, in those cases, be sure to list some specific examples. Furthermore, start with positive language when you can. For example, you may want to allow side hugs for children who need consoling. So, you could say that side hugs, when the child wants hugs, are an example of good mentoring, but any other contact is inappropriate. Some codes of contact for older children and teens simply say that the only acceptable zones of contact are around/above the shoulders and on the arms. Think through what your program needs and what specific definitions you can give your staff and volunteers. Be as specific as you can while also being thorough.

Use age-appropriate rules. Be aware of the standards of care for the ages of the children you serve. For example, many groups at one time prohibited all physical contact between staff and children. Childcare centers, however, gradually realized that young children not only want healthy physical contact but also need it for normal healthy development. So, most groups that work with preschool children now encourage staff to respond warmly when children initiate hugs or other physical contact. Most early education programs do add restrictions as children get older—such as discouraging lap-sitting for older preschool students, both because it can be inappropriate and because it can signal favoritism. Any boundary rules, however, must be geared to the age and normal development of the children in the program.

Another area that you need to consider if you have infants and younger toddlers is hygiene rules. Children who are not potty-trained will need help from staff. Think through what your rules will be about who can help them and how someone else can monitor the interactions. You may be able to require open bathroom doors, for example, for younger toddlers, but older children who express privacy concerns may require Dutch doors that close at the bottom.

Have clear consequences for boundary violations. Be sure that the consequences for violating codes of conduct are very clear for your staff. Consider whether to set out a rule that repeated violations will warrant more severe discipline, up to and including termination for employment. You also may want to distinguish between accidental, reckless, and intentional violations of policy.

We do recommend that you avoid "zero-tolerance" rules. It sounds good to say that a given policy is so important that any violation (even accidental) will result in getting fired, but zero-tolerance rules generally will cause you more trouble than they are worth. First, decades of experience with policies have shown that staff are more reluctant to report violations if they believe reporting will get their coworkers fired. Second, it's very hard to be consistent in administering draconian policies that seem unfair in a given situation. People who work with children tend to be kind-hearted, and it's much easier to give a worker a second chance than to enforce a zero-tolerance rule. However, if there are no consequences to a rule violation, then in reality, there's no rule.

In actual practice, it works much better to distinguish between accidental, reckless, and intentional violation of a policy. We cover these principles and practices in Chapter 8. They are an important part of creating a solid safety culture in your organization.

Evaluate frequent code violations. If you start seeing frequent violations of a particular rule, then you need to figure out why. If people are ignoring the rule without consequences, then obviously the rule might as well not exist. On the other hand, if you are disciplining a lot of workers for violating a rule, then maybe that rule isn't working for your program. Take a hard look at your codes of conduct to be sure that they are working for you and making your program better.

IN-PROGRAM INTERACTIONS

Your program likely already has rules about interactions between adults and minors within your program. As you evaluate and tweak those rules, look at these common areas where we've seen problems arise for youth organizations.

Physical Contact

Most organizations recognize the need for these rules, and the details will depend on the parameters of your particular program. As we explained above, you need clear rules governing physical contact between adults and minors. Be sure that your rules are age-appropriate and consistently enforceable.

Conversations and Communications

Be sure that your conduct rules cover the language that your workers use when talking to minors. Research what standards your state law uses for emotional abuse as well as sexual harassment. Also draw a strict boundary against suggestive language, as pushing limits in sexual-oriented conversation is one of the hallmarks of predatory grooming. Use positive language as much as possible but be clear about your expectations.

Gifts and Favoritism

Be sure that your rules prohibit more than token gifts as well as any behavior that looks like favoritism from adults. For example, if your teachers send birthday cards, require them to send a card to every child in the class. One of the hallmarks of predatory grooming behavior is singling out a child for special attention. You need clear boundaries to prevent that behavior and catch any violations early.

Minor Workers

It's easy to forget that some interns or volunteers also are minors. Be sure that you enforce your boundary rules for your workers, just the same as you do for the minors that you serve in your program.

Two-Adult Rule

It's common to see advice that you have a rule requiring two adults to be with every group of minors. In our experience, that rule works very well for groups that depend on volunteers such as churches or scouting programs. For organizations that depend on employees, however, it can be problematic. Few YSOs can afford to hire twice as many staff as they need.

If your budget doesn't allow two workers for each group of minors, consider using enhanced supervision and line-of-sight rules instead. For example, require that classroom doors always be open to allow a clear line of sight for people walking by. If you plan renovations, consider wide windows in interior walls and doors to allow for a clear view into rooms. Be sure that administrators "supervise by walking around" with impromptu and random checks. Be particularly certain to have frequent checks of isolated areas such as bathrooms.

Prohibition on 1:1 Contact

Another common piece of advice is to prohibit all one-on-one contact between adults and minors. Again, this advice works better for some organizations than others. Schools, for example, may find that teachers need to meet individually with students who are having trouble mastering classroom material. Rules for mental health counselors often require privacy, meaning that it's impossible to include anyone else in the meetings. Mentoring organizations by definition involve more individual than group interactions. If your organization needs to allow periodic one-on-one meetings during your program, think through what supervision you can provide. In addition to the examples above, consider requiring advanced notice for tutoring sessions. Mentoring groups can encourage group activities or use the rules we mention below for in-home contact. Have your CST search for creative, but workable, ways to allow your workers to do their jobs while discouraging predatory behavior.

OUT-OF-PROGRAM INTERACTIONS

One area that many youth organizations overlook is out-of-program contact. In the next section, we'll discuss contact through social media or correspondence. Before we get to that, let's look at in-person contacts. As litigation against youth organizations has accelerated in past years, we've seen more cases involving behavior that happened when parents were supposed to be supervising the victim. Courts have allowed claims that the parents reasonably thought that the program had vouched for the worker and trusted the predator more than they would have otherwise. Therefore, to fully protect both your organization and the children in your care, you need clear rules for contact between your workers and minor children outside the bounds of your program.

Babysitting

One common area that youth programs face is whether parents can hire workers to babysit. Some organizations simply prohibit babysitting, but smaller organizations find that so many parents and workers are friends outside the program that reasonable exceptions swallow up the rule. As with all the other policies we discuss in this book, *only set a rule you can consistently enforce.* For example, if there's no way for you to learn on a regular basis whether your workers are babysitting, or if prohibiting babysitting would deprive you of good workers, then there's no point in having a rule against it. Seasonal camps sometimes will find out after camp is over that parents have invited cabin counselors to go on family vacations. The only leverage the camps have in that situation is to not rehire the counselor, but it doesn't prevent the contact. Fortunately, there are ways that you can protect your program in those situations.

First, be sure that whatever policy you have is written clearly in both your staff and parent handbooks. If you can't prevent outside contact, but you want to discourage it, say that you discourage it. If you prohibit it, let parents know that by asking a staff member to babysit, they are asking the employee to put his or her job on the line. If you allow it, but require advance notice, then let both the employees and parents know that they need to make arrangements early. Whatever parameters you set up, communicate them clearly in your documentation to everyone who might be involved.

Second, let parents know that supervising and screening any worker who provides services to the family outside the program is the *parents'* responsibility. If your state allows you to require releases and waivers, put that language in whatever parent handbook or contract that your parents sign. Consult with a lawyer in your jurisdiction about what language the courts will uphold if there are problems.

Finally, if your program serves teenagers, discourage your workers from using those young people for babysitting, housework, or other work at your employees' or volunteers' homes. Put that language in both staff handbooks and parent handbooks. Also, put in your agreement with the teens' parents whatever language your jurisdiction allows that makes it clear that, if the parents allow their children to work for your staff, the parents are taking total responsibility for that arrangement.

In-Home Mentoring and Tutoring

A similar situation arises when workers are providing services, such as tutoring or therapy, at the children's homes. Mentoring organizations usually do most of their work in groups or at the mentee's home. In either situation, follow the principles set out above as they apply to the situation. In addition, require the parents to be present and within earshot at all times. Put that requirement in both your workers' and your parents' agreements.

Think through what your employee or volunteer should do if parents say they are running to the store for a bit or are otherwise out of earshot. Give your workers the tools they need to avoid claims that they were alone with youth and that something bad happened.

Transportation

Sometimes parents will ask staff or volunteers to transport students to and from practices and meetings. If you can't practically prohibit this routine, then at least include transportation in whatever waivers you can get parents to sign. Also seriously consider screening those workers for their driving record so that you can either prohibit them from driving children or warn parents about their record.

Some youth organizations rely on parents to provide transportation to sporting events or competitions. Consult with your lawyer about language for the agreement with parents. It needs to be clear that the parents are responsible for providing transportation for their children, and that, if they are relying on other parents for transport, they are solely responsible for screening and supervising those parents.

These are only a few of the common examples of in-person interactions that we have seen outside youth programs. As part of evaluating or writing your policies, think through the contacts that your workers are likely to have with the youth in your care and develop realistic policies for dealing with them.

SOCIAL MEDIA AND CORRESPONDENCE

A uniquely problematic area of off-campus contact is social media, email, and other correspondence. It's an area where you can encourage positive communications. Several children in our families, for example, were thrilled to receive cards from counselors welcoming them to day camps. Group chats and email lists can be a great way to build morale among team members or classrooms. Social media groups can help keep campers tied into seasonal camps and coming back in later years.

As with all adult-child communications, however, you need to protect both the children and your organization. Consider the following principles and ideas to see which will work for your organization.

Include social media and correspondence in your content rules. We discussed above that you need rules to protect minors from harassment, bullying, and other inappropriate conversations. Be clear in your handbooks and codes of conduct that these rules apply to communications both inside and outside your program, in person and online.

Prohibit individual (one-on-one) interactions on social media. Social media can be either a great tool for your organization or a serious liability. The best protection that we have found is to prohibit individual friending and following on personal social media accounts. Allowing staff to individually follow students on TikTok or any other social media platform blurs boundaries between professionals and students. Individual interactions also are impossible for you to monitor. The same applies with allowing students to "follow" or "friend" staff. As noted below, your organization's social media accounts can follow different rules.

Finally, in our experience, emotionally healthy adults generally appreciate this particular boundary. Most adults don't particularly want to have minors as part of their personal social media experience. Younger adults may not know quite how to make the transition from teen to adult leader, and a restriction on social media is a good guardrail for them. In either instance, a bright-line rule makes it easier for workers to deny a child's request.

Limit individual communications to approved program platforms. There may be many good reasons for an adult in your program to communicate individually with a minor. A schoolteacher doesn't need to include the entire class in an email discussion about one student's homework problems, for example. Similarly, a child may reach out to a trusted adult about a personal problem, and we don't want to completely isolate children from healthy relationships with trusted adults. The best way to encourage those healthy communications is to require that they only happen via your program's email server or other approved platform. This requirement allows administrators in your program to have a record of the communications and to check them at any time. This level of transparency is essential to a good child protection program.

Monitor program-related social media or email groups. Many organizations find that social media groups help build a strong community. Camps, for example, often use social media groups for alumni as a way of building enthusiasm year after year. Extra-curricular groups in schools find that group emails or apps are an efficient way to communicate. If you decide that a social media group or email list could benefit your program, be certain that an administrator is included. Then be sure that the administrator monitors it periodically. The administrator needs to not only enforce content rules but also to watch for problematic behavior. If an adult, for example, suggests that a conversation be taken outside the group, then the administrator needs to know why. There may be a good reason, such as a student's disclosing trauma or abuse, in which case the administrator needs to become part of the conversation. What does not need to happen is an adult's isolating a child from the group, even electronically.

Consider requiring that workers include parents or administrators in emails. In most organizations, it isn't practical for administrators to read every email that workers send to minors in the program. If your organization is small enough, then definitely consider taking advantage of the transparency that comes from including an administrator in communications. But if it's not practical, then don't set yourself up for failure with a rule that you can't follow. Instead, consider requiring that workers copy parents on all their emails. Parents generally will have both more time and personal motivation to keep up with who is saying what to their kids.

If the conversation is one that the kids want to keep private from their parents, then you can require that an administrator be copied or blind copied. That category will be a smaller, probably more manageable number. More importantly, if the issue is a serious one, such as a disclosure of abuse, then an administrator will need to be involved anyway.

Have a clear rule about texting. Decide what rule you want to have about texting between adults and minors. In most organizations, there will not be a legitimate need for adults to text children, and you can include it in the prohibition against individual communications. If you do see a need, then try to find ways to limit and monitor the communications. For example, if workers are taking a group of teens on a field trip, you may need to have text messaging set up as a safety measure. In that case, consider whether it's practical to get each staff member a prepaid phone or whether you can limit communications to an application that you can record and monitor. Other organizations have required group texting, applying the same rules that prohibit 1:1 emails. There is no single solution to the texting conundrum. Simply be sure that you have analyzed the problem and done the best job you can to balance the competing safety concerns.

Communicate the rules to parents. Finally, be sure that you have clearly communicated these rules to your parents. Parents generally are the best supervisors of their children, and they are much more likely than anyone else to notice problematic communications. Furthermore, simply having the information in the parents' handbook adds a level of transparency that can deter bad behavior from an adult. Don't overlook this powerful resource for your child protection program.

"DON'T TELL MY PARENTS!"

Children and youth in your program may develop a trusting relationship with an adult worker in your program and may desire to confide in the adult some problem they are having that they do not want shared with parents: a personal conflict with a friend, pressure to drink or use drugs, an emerging eating disorder, or abuse at home. While we want our programs to be places of support for these youth, it's critically important to set expectations for when your staff can hold a youth's confidences. Allegations of abuse by a parent, for example, almost always must be reported. And increasingly, withholding important information from parents about a child's emotional or mental health struggles has resulted in lawsuits against YSOs. In many jurisdictions, parents have certain rights to be notified about issues involving their own children unless the child is reporting abuse, or disclosure to the parent raises a significant danger to the child's physical or emotional health. Consult with your attorney on appropriate guidelines for when a child's statements can be held in confidence, and make sure that you clearly outline those rules in your parent and student handbooks and in your staff training.

UNDERSTAND THE DIFFERENCE BETWEEN HEALTHY MENTORING AND PREDATORY GROOMING

We have mentioned several times the importance of protecting children against grooming by predators. Grooming occurs when adults use flattery and charm to break down a child's natural barriers and gradually introduce the child to sexual behavior. It is a serious risk that all youth organizations need to guard against.

The problem is that the characteristics used to describe both good mentors and predatory groomers are often similar, making it hard to tell the difference from outside the relationship. We've had numerous clients say, "Until we found out about the abuse, we thought he was the best staff member we had ever had." Predators tend to be charming and very good at connecting with both kids and parents.

Youth organizations need to be vigilant, but not at the cost of losing good mentors. Research in childhood trauma shows that the single most common factor in building resilience is for a child to have a strong and healthy relationship with a caring adult. Ironically, this means that being overly protective of children to the point that we deprive them of good mentors actually can cause its own level of harm.

Avoiding grooming behavior while encouraging mentoring behavior requires that you pay attention to the unique characteristics of harmful grooming. Those red flags are (1) favoritism, (2) isolation, and (3) boundary violations. In short, creating and maintaining strong boundary lines in the relationship distinguishes healthy mentoring from harmful grooming.

Favoritism

Avoiding favoritism is a hallmark of good professional behavior. Children don't need to feel that a staff member plays favorites, even if the child benefits from being the favorite. If you notice a staff member setting up a strong relationship with a child or group of children, then you need to pay attention to those dynamics.

Of course, people tend to have personality types that they get along with better than others. Some adults gravitate to problem kids, while others gravitate to young people with particular interests. You can't change human nature, and you can seriously damage employee morale if you start micromanaging normal human tendencies. What you are looking for is not adults who have a soft spot for a particular troublemaker or get along better with one child than another. Rather, you are looking for favoritism that is beyond the bounds of normal professional interactions.

One common example of favoritism would be a staff member providing expensive gifts or spending an unusual amount of time and resources on a child. There's no doubt that our programs will encounter children who need resources, and youth workers often have a soft spot for children in need. We have all heard heartwarming stories of teachers or mentors who became foster parents for children that they met in a YSO. What distinguishes those stories from grooming situations is that the good mentors followed the procedure of an established program and went through all the necessary screening. They didn't insert themselves into a child's life without oversight or accountability. In other words, they recognized boundaries while providing critical help.

If you see problematic favoritism for a child who has a legitimate need, remind your worker of appropriate boundaries. Then try to find help from a reputable source that will remove your organization and your kind-hearted worker from the equation. How the worker responds to the communication of these limits will tell you a lot of what you need to know about their intentions.

If you are operating a program that serves children or youth experiencing significant poverty or who are living in a very poor neighborhood, region, or nation, you should consider establishing rules regarding when, how, and whether staff, volunteers, donors, mentors, or other adults may bring gifts to children. When not handled properly, such gift-giving can create not only an appearance of favoritism but also can create conflict between the children participating in the program and others in the community.

Isolation

Predators tend to isolate their victims, either physically or emotionally. Line of sight and other rules discussed above are important to prevent physical isolation. You also need to pay attention to emotional isolation. It's very common for predators to tell kids that no one else understands them or cares for them as much as or in the same way that the predator does. We also frequently see groomers encourage children to keep things secret from their parents or other adults. This tendency toward isolation is one reason that you should consider having a parent or administrator copied on emails. This practice makes it difficult for a worker to keep secrets from parents or supervisors, unless done so deliberately.

Boundary Violations

The third characteristic that you often see is boundary violations. People intent on grooming a child will push the boundaries of professional behavior and start inserting themselves into personal areas. In the screening section, we mentioned one example where an adult engages with a student as a peer. This level of unprofessionalism doesn't always mean that the adult is a pedophile. Sometimes young adults really do see themselves as peers of older teens, and new adults can drift into serious problems before they realize it. In these cases, clear boundaries protect both the minor and the young staff member.

More often, though, we see predators deliberately testing boundaries or overstepping them. Of course, violation of physical boundaries is always a red flag. Conversations also can create boundary issues, such as when a worker shares inappropriate details about his or her personal life or steers the conversation toward sexually oriented topics. Similarly, soliciting information about a student's personal life (outside a professional counseling setting) should raise concerns.

We often see boundary violations coupled with isolation and/ or favoritism. One scenario that we often see is a worker encouraging minors to watch pornography with him or her and then keep it a secret from anyone else. Predators instinctively know that encouraging children and teens to engage in edgy behavior breaks down their natural resistance to abuse, while keeping it a secret isolates them from adults who could help them. These patterns are common among predators because, unfortunately, they work.

When you see boundary violations, you must deal with them immediately and thoroughly. As we discuss in Chapter 8, not every violation warrants terminating the worker. Serious boundary violations, however, or a pattern of violations usually indicates that this person should not be allowed access to the children in your program.

These three issues are not the only indicators of grooming, but almost every situation will have one of these red flags. Watch for them so that you can encourage healthy relationships between your workers and the kids in your program and you can weed out the dangerous adults.

Remember also that limiting or prohibiting contact outside the program, as discussed above, is a significant tool in your efforts to prevent isolation, favoritism, and boundary violations. Within international child and youth-serving programs, for example, organizations have experienced situations in which a child sponsor was able to use the information about a child provided by the organization to contact, groom, and abuse the child.

YOUTH CODES OF CONDUCT

It's easy to concentrate on avoiding predatory adults and forget that minors victimizing each other is a more common problem. So, your codes of conduct need to address that behavior in addition to the usual rules about attendance and activities. Consider whether rules about the following areas need to be in your documentation.

Encourage and reward positive interactions. Just as with staff codes of conduct, use positive language wherever you can. It's not practical to do this exclusively, but at least try to lead with positive language. This can be particularly important at younger ages, because up to a certain point, children can be naturally cruel to each other. Part of our job is to teach them the concepts of respect, kindness, and empathy. Aspirational statements can be a good place to start.

Use clear rules with examples. Clear language and examples are even more important for minors than for adults. Younger children think concretely and tend to learn best from clear examples. Even as children grow older, they need clear language to be able to understand expectations. We can't just assume that they know what "kindness" means or looks like in practice; we need to give them a clear model for their behavior.

It's tempting to use vague language because it leaves our options open when we must deal with problems. Vagueness, however, is not fair to children who are still learning societal norms, the boundaries of acceptable behavior, and how to control impulses. Fairness is particularly important for emotionally charged concepts with changing definitions, such as harassment or hate speech or inappropriate contact. If we want kids to avoid certain behavior, we must teach them what it looks like before they stumble into it.

Cover in-program technology use. Be sure that your rules are clear about acceptable use of technology in your program. For technology that you provide in your program, such as computer labs, have clear rules about what content the minors can access. Of course, your IT department should also install filters, but you can't rely just on technology alone. Many older children and teenagers are surprisingly adept at working around filters, whether innocently or maliciously. Have clear boundaries and remind your workers to enforce them.

Cover the use of personal technology within your program. Many of our clients prohibit personal smartphones, tablets, and computers within their program. If parents complain that their children need phones as a safety measure, you could consider allowing only flip phones. If you don't think you can completely prohibit technology, then set clear restrictions on when students can access it and what content they can access.

Prohibit bullying and cyberbullying. Many state laws now require schools to have rules about bullying, and Title IX requires any program that receives federal funds to protect minors from sexual harassment. Even if you don't have such laws governing your organization, you still need to protect your students from either in-person or online bullying. This sort of victimization has always been a problem, and it has become a much bigger mental health issue in the age of social media.

As we noted above and explain in the next point, however, it's not enough to simply say "no bullying." This term has become so common that it now can mean anything, which amounts to meaning practically nothing. Look for specific definitions in the statutes or regulations that govern your programs. Even if you aren't required to include particular language, you may find these definitions helpful in distinguishing between actual bullying and ordinary thoughtless behavior by clueless kids.

One definition that many organizations use as a starting point is the CDC's definition, which focuses on (1) repeated events, (2) intentional and aggressive behaviors, and (3) situations where there is a significant power imbalance between the parties. You can find this definition by searching for "bullying" on the CDC website, www.cdc.gov.

Distinguish between bullying and conflict. Even while you have rules against bullying, you must distinguish between true bullying and ordinary conflict. The main reason it's important to differentiate between bullying and ordinary conflict is that conflict in itself isn't all bad. People always will have their own preferences, and being free to express those is part of being an emotionally healthy adult. Always suppressing opinions to avoid conflict is not a good way to build a relationship.

Furthermore, interpersonal conflicts are a normal part of life, and children will never be able to avoid peer conflict. It will be a part of their everyday experience as adults, whether in the workplace or in their personal relationships. They will graduate from childhood conflict to workplace conflict, so they need to learn basic social skills now to deal with those differences later. Dealing with conflict in a gracious and positive manner is an important skill, and the sooner they learn that life skill, the happier they will be.

It's also important to understand the distinct differences involved in handling normal arguments versus bullying behaviors. Conflict resolution strategies will help solve ordinary conflicts. School or workplace bullying, however, requires stronger boundaries and usually action from upper management—action that would be overkill for minor conflicts. Conversely, asking young people to "work it out" in a bullying situation will only make the situation worse. We need to be able to apply different solutions to different situations.

Distinguishing between bullying and conflict doesn't mean that you discourage the children from reporting disputes. It does mean that you need to respond to each problem differently. Be clear in your rules and among your workers about which behavior is grounds for discipline, and which warrants correction and teaching.

Decide what out-of-program behavior your conduct code covers. Finally, be sure you decide what out-of-program behavior you should try to manage. Some organizations lack the resources to police outside behavior, while others can impose restrictions. Your rule also may be affected by your parents' expectations. For example, parents often expect schools to take action about more outside behavior than they do other organizations, particularly if it is bullying that is affecting the child's ability to learn on campus.

Behavior that affects your program is a good dividing line, and one that is rapidly becoming very common. Consider whether you want to reserve the right to respond to outside behavior that is affecting your ability to serve the minors in your program. If you do, then state it clearly in your code of conduct.

PHYSICAL FACILITY

Finally, analyze whether you can make affordable changes to your physical facility to enhance your child protection. Look for ways that you can address the common problem areas of line of sight and secluded areas.

First, take a long look at whether you can increase your ability to see interactions in your program, whether between adults and minors or between minors. Perhaps you need more windows in your interior walls or doors. If you have younger children who need help with toileting, consider Dutch doors that allow adults (but not other children) to peer in. Be sure that your policy prohibits artwork or curtains on any of the windows in the walls or doors. Walk through your physical plant to see what obstructions exist to a clear line of sight and investigate what changes you can make within your budget.

Second, determine how to deal with secluded areas that you can't change. For example, you can't have windows in bathroom walls. Storage closets usually don't have windows in the doors; consider how you will prevent a predator from using that area to harm a child. Also, remember to have the ability to open closet doors from the inside without a key so that children don't get trapped in there.

If you don't have the budget to make physical changes or if your privacy rules require some level of seclusion, then be sure that your policy includes enhanced supervision. Assign workers to check bathrooms frequently, for example, and have administrators randomly and frequently check rooms that your program is using. These practices are a good idea even if you can make the physical facility meet your ideal, but they are essential when your budget limits the renovations you can make.

Behavior and boundary guidelines may be the most vexing of your policies to write and enforce, but they are often the most important. Draft policies so that you can recognize problems before they grow into crises, and deal with them before someone causes serious damage to minors and to your program.

CHAPTER 8

CREATING A STRONG SAFETY CULTURE

NOW THAT YOU have written a good child protection policy, how do you make sure it becomes an accepted and seamless part of your program? In our experience, for YSOs to successfully implement child safety requires building an *organizational culture* that supports child and youth safety. Building a "safety culture" within your organization is just as important as—and sometimes even more important than—having the right written policies.

SAFETY CULTURE: BRINGING ENGINEERING SAFETY TO CHILD PROTECTION

Think of an industry in which professionals make high-risk decisions every day. They can't afford mistakes and can't "learn by failing," because a failure might lead to a death. When something goes wrong, the results might be catastrophic. What industry were you thinking of? Airlines? Nuclear Energy? Neurosurgery? How about human services? Child and youth serving-organizations?

Human services organizations have a mission to serve *and protect* clients and beneficiaries. You can't do that if your organization is not a safe place for staff, volunteers, and especially for the children and youth you serve. No matter what policies you have in place, if you don't create an organizational culture in which safety for staff, volunteers, and youth is part of the fabric, your policies will fail.

For that reason, service organizations should adopt a "just" or "safety" culture. This is a culture that emphasizes both child safety and accounting for ordinary human error.

WHAT IS JUST/SAFETY CULTURE?

Over the past few years, many YSOs have re-energized their efforts to safeguard the children and vulnerable adults they serve from abuse and sexual exploitation. Many NGOs have adopted zero-tolerance policies for harassment, abuse, and exploitation. But safeguarding scandals continue, and even strenuous efforts haven't been effective in stopping them. One problem is that many organizations have taken a centralized, top-down approach, focusing on policies and compliance, reporting mandates, and HQ-led investigations.

Safety culture, by contrast, assumes that people will err, and that most errors don't actually lead to harmful outcomes. In a compliance-driven culture, action is usually taken only when there is a bad result or harm. In a safety culture, the organization focuses on ensuring that risky behavior is hard to get away with, is reported, and is acted upon in a way that reduces risk.

Just culture, or safety culture, is an approach to organizational culture-building that grew out of efforts to figure out what went wrong in the Space Shuttle *Challenger* disaster of 1986. Investigators found that faulty O-rings that were supposed to contain hot gases failed due to cold weather. The resulting leak ignited a fire that resulted in the shuttle's exploding in midair, killing six astronauts and one civilian teacher.

After the tragedy, a safety review found that engineers had known about the potential problem with the O-rings for quite some time. Lower-level engineering staff knew the O-rings became stiff at lower temperatures and had cautioned against launching the shuttle in cold weather. Middle management overruled the decision, and no one else spoke up, leaving launch control unaware of the risks of a cold-weather countdown. NASA had developed an organizational culture in which management ignored knowledgeable employees and stymied criticism. In other words, the problem was a cultural one. Because the organization ignored known risks, staff became complacent to the point that they actually believed there was no risk.

The safety culture concepts from that engineering disaster entered the field of medicine with the 1999 publication of *To Err is Human: Building a Safer Health System*, a deep review of why almost 100,000 people died each year from preventable medical errors. The study concluded that most medical errors resulted from systems that did not account for human frailty. The problem was not a particular medical professional, but systemic errors and poor organizational culture. From that work came a set of "just culture" or "safety culture" principles now widely applied in hospitals and other medical settings.

In groundbreaking work at Vanderbilt University Medical Center, the concept of safety culture was applied to the problem of hospital-acquired infections. Each year, hospital officials were finding that many patients were becoming sick because physicians making rounds were not washing their hands between seeing patients. Hospital orderlies and nurses were observing these failures, but were afraid to speak up for fear of retribution for "criticizing" their superiors.

The problem couldn't be isolated to one person's failure. The culture of the hospital contributed to it. Doctors got lazy about washing their hands. The hierarchy made it difficult for lower-status employees to speak up. To correct the problem, Vanderbilt changed not its policies but rather its culture. The hospital made it clear that it was the job of every staff member to ensure good handwashing. Lower-level employees were encouraged to and expected to speak up if they saw a physician skip the handwashing protocols. Physicians found in violation were not disciplined but rather were held accountable through a conversation with hospital safety officers. Infection rates plummeted.

NORMALIZED DEVIANCE: THE TRAP OF COMPLACENCY

How do these engineering and medical principles apply to youth organizations? They show that we must create a work climate that recognizes and combats the human tendency to get tired of following top-down rules, including our child protection policies.

Think back to the early days of the Covid-19 pandemic. People were conscientious about wearing masks. Everyone took social distancing seriously, and many took to heart the advice to sing "Happy Birthday" twice while washing their hands. But after a while, we saw others wearing masks below their noses. Everyone missed the good old days of sitting around a table with friends. Even while the illness was still a threat, many people got tired of following the strenuous rules. We developed what engineers call "normalized deviance," or what some people refer to as "compliance fatigue." The same phenomenon can quickly transform a YSO full of good people intent on protecting youth into one in which young people suffer abuse, injury, or exploitation.

For example, consider the typical policy of preventing staff and volunteers from being alone with children. That basic rule makes common sense. One doesn't have to be an expert to understand that an adult who seeks to abuse or exploit a child will likely try to isolate that child. So, imagine that, as an organization director, you are sitting in your office alone one afternoon when an 8-year-old child comes running into your office with tears in his eyes, slams the door behind him and tells you that he fell down on the playground and scratched his knee. He wants a band-aid and a hug.

If your first reaction is to immediately open the office door and call for another adult to come monitor you, you may not be a real human. In such situations, adults who care about children will usually first attend to the child's needs. In the world of written policy, you would have to report yourself to human resources. In the real world, you'd ensure the child gets safely back to the playground with his knee cleaned and covered with a fresh Band-aid.

But think of the many daily interactions between staff or volunteers and children and multiply many times over your moment of making care a priority. What happens to the rule? If you as the director are flexible with this rule, other employees will likely follow suit. They may forget to ensure another adult is present or nearby when they need to have a private counseling session with a child. They may allow children to sit in their laps, forgetting the required space they are supposed to maintain between themselves and children. Faced with a rigid rule that may be impractical to enforce, staff and volunteers may begin to ignore the rule entirely, until one day an offender takes advantage of the lax atmosphere to isolate and molest a child or youth.

In technical terms, this process of slouching toward laxity is known as "normalized deviance," a term coined by sociologist Diane Vaughn in her review of the Challenger disaster. In practice, the following factors contribute to the phenomenon:

1. **Staff or volunteers consider a rule impractical.** They may think of it as "stupid," or imposed from above with no understanding of how things operate on the ground daily.

2. **The rule is not clear, so different people apply it differently.** Sometimes insufficient or ineffective training leads to exceptions that swallow up the original rule. In watching and learning from veteran staff, new employees and volunteers may pick up a version of the rule that is far from the one written in handbooks.

3. **The work involves good reasons to break the rule, providing an incentive for shortcuts.** (In the example above, what could be more important than immediately attending to a child's needs?)

4. **Staff begin to feel that the rules don't really apply to them.** They think, "I'm here to care for children, not exploit them. This rule is intended to stop pedophiles."

5. **Staff and volunteers are afraid to speak up when they see the rule violated.** If everyone is breaking the rule, including the director, they ask themselves, "Who am I to stick my neck out?" Similarly, zero-tolerance policies leave staff unwilling to see a colleague fired for a technical violation.

6. **Leadership doesn't acknowledge the situation.** They prefer to leave unchallenged their message that "we are in full compliance with our child protection policies."

NORMALIZED DEVIANCE LEADS TO SYSTEMIC FAILURES

One of the brightest minds on the issue of handling human services system failures is British expert Eileen Munro. As she has noted, tragic failures in other systems—whether it's a plane crash, a collapsing bridge or a patient who dies at the hospital—rarely involve one major mistake by one person. Rather, she writes, these tragedies result from many small system errors, most of them harmless by themselves but disastrous when combined. Thus, firing the person who made the final mistake does not solve the problem. We must examine the entire system to address all of the small flaws.

The two critical elements you need to institute a just culture or safety culture in your organization are (1) psychological safety and (2) positive accountability.

COMBATTING NORMALIZED DEVIANCE: CREATING PSYCHOLOGICAL SAFETY

"Psychological safety" is a sense among your workers that they are free to speak up without fear of retaliation. It is the voluntary *reporting* of policy violations or errors that allows the organization and its leadership to understand whether its policies are being followed, whether they are effective, and whether they improve child safety. Most errors and policy violations *don't* result in harm to a child. But due to the phenomenon of normalized deviance, when a policy violation doesn't result in harm to a child, staff often do not report the breach. Why? It's human nature.

In many organizations, as in much of life, individuals don't want to call out their colleagues. That hesitation starts in childhood, when teachers, parents or even other children tell us, "Don't be a tattletale." As adults, we face the same bias against telling on co-workers, except we use more advanced labels, such as "gossip," "troublemaker," and "busybody." The retaliation that workers fear can range from official job discipline to being shunned by colleagues.

When normalized deviance collides with the social consequences of being labeled a "tattletale," policy compliance goes downhill with no repercussions until policy violations explode in a scandal. The organization must create a work environment where reporting policy violations is as normal and as socially accepted as filling out an expense form. Building psychological safety can help achieve that goal.

Before building your organization's psychological safety, you need to know how safe employees and volunteers *currently* feel.

That's the point of the annual audit in Worksheets #3 and #4 that we recommend. The Psychological Safety Inventory will tell you where you need to start in building a safe culture for a strong child protection policy.

Once you get the results of that survey, the difficult part begins. Creating psychological safety requires leaders to *ask* staff questions, to *listen* to staff, and to *demonstrate* they listened by responding. It requires constant communication between and among all levels of the organization and puts the burden on leaders to adopt a grassroots approach in which they regularly seek input from those closest to the work. If you see problems in your survey results, that's where you need to start focusing your practices and procedures.

Building Psychological Safety

As you try to build psychological safety among your team members, consider how the following principles would look in your organization.

Clarify how you will address violations of policy. How does your organization currently address policy violations? Will the HR director and a witness come to the employee's office or workplace and interview them? Will you promise confidentiality, despite the fact that other staff members know that something is going on? What do your policies currently say about the consequences of a violation? Many child protection policies emphasize "zero-tolerance" for child maltreatment and state that violations can result in discipline "up to and including termination." Exactly what does that mean in a given situation?

Be sure your policies explain at least (1) *who* will respond (which may vary depending on the type of violation); (2) *how* the appropriate staff will address an alleged violation, with details on the fact-finding process, whether the matter will be handled internally or an outside evaluator brought in, the extent of confidentiality, and potential penalties for failing to cooperate, recognizing that different levels of violation may require different responses; and (3) *types* of accountability, categorized by the severity of a violation.

Use collaborative language over adversarial. In our experience, the vast majority of people who work with youth and other vulnerable populations are well-intentioned, sensitive, and kind. Many youth organizations, however, present their child protection policies as a threat. Use collaborative language as much as possible when writing your policies, when discussing how you will implement them, and when addressing an incident.

Avoid letting the situation become personal. It is natural for individuals to become defensive when they are challenged. They tend to misrepresent or "misremember" their actions, deflect blame to others, and minimize bad outcomes. Individuals who are secure in their place and identity within a group are much less likely to become defensive when told they have erred.

A healthy work relationship, like any other relationship, is built on trust. And trust is something that must be built over time *before* the need arises for a difficult conversation, whether that conversation is a dispute between husband and wife about finances or a conversation about work performance between an employee and a supervisor. As a leader, start building that trust now, *before* you need to engage in a difficult conversation about work performance. Your relationship with that worker needs to be sufficiently solid so that he or she will trust your motives and receive your criticism the way you intend it. If not, you will have to find someone else in the organization who has that relationship with the worker.

Build a record of acknowledging your own flaws and mistakes. If there is one quality that is most conducive to building psychological safety, it's humility. You don't have to demonstrate humility through some sort of Maoist struggle session. Rather, leaders can demonstrate humility by regularly asking questions and acknowledging they don't have all the answers, by regularly inviting input and feedback from staff at all levels, by *acknowledging that feedback*, and by expressing curiosity about new ideas.

POSITIVE ACCOUNTABILITY

Safety culture also requires both individual and *organizational* accountability. This is because, while humans make errors, the organization has a responsibility to design systems that reduce the likelihood of those errors. Accountability in a just culture does not simply involve discipline or consequences; rather, leadership must design a system that is accountable to employees while also holding employees (and volunteers and participants) accountable to the system. Worksheet #4 is a survey to help you determine how your workers view the accountability in your program.

In a safety culture, it's important for individuals to *self-report* mistakes, errors, and concerns, especially when they don't lead to actual harm, so that leadership can both determine whether any discipline is necessary *and* determine whether there were systemic issues that led to the issue. Having the courage to report one's own mistakes requires an environment of psychological safety, as mentioned above. Employees need to know that if they report their concerns and even their own errors, leadership will not take a punitive approach but will instead work with them to see how the *system* can be improved to reduce human error.

The Problem with Punishment

How do employees know that when they report concerns about themselves or others, their leadership will support and listen to them and act on their concerns? Here are three methods to create such an environment.

A grassroots approach works better than a top-down one. Staff on the front lines are best situated to spot inappropriate behavior before it results in harm, but these staff are often the least likely to speak up or to be heard. In youth-serving organizations, secondary trauma, burnout, and the urgency of the work can contribute to a culture that tolerates risky behavior. Staff in the field may resent being mandated to follow practices they had no hand in developing. Hierarchical reporting systems and work structures can also impede reporting. Because risky or inappropriate behavior can become normalized, staff in the field must feel ownership of safeguarding duties. Instilling that ownership requires involving field staff in the development and testing of policies and requesting regular feedback from them on how their safeguarding efforts are faring.

A non-punitive response is critical when it is an available option. Abuse and exploitation are emotional issues that trigger emotional reactions. To prevent actual harm, staff must feel confident that if they intervene to *stop* inappropriate behavior, then the organization's response will be measured. Most actual abuse of children occurs at the end of a longer process in which the offender is allowed to break boundaries, make inappropriate comments, and slowly isolate the victim. Field staff who see these warning signs need to feel that, if they report them, the organization will respond in a way that preserves the local working team while holding the wrongdoer accountable. Organizations should create tiers of responses, clearly describe for the field what types of actions or behavior workers should report, and demonstrate that responses to risky behavior will be corrected in a way that does not damage local working relationships. Actual abuse or exploitation, on the other hand, should result in quick and decisive discipline.

Supportive leadership is the final and perhaps most important element. In each of the child protection scandals that we have witnessed, there were incidents, rumors, and concerns that the organization did not address long before the scandal became public. Leadership responses to those prior situations often revealed two common themes. Either the organization had fired a few "bad apples" and "moved on," or the leadership had stuck its head in the sand for fear of having information revealed that could damage the organization's reputation. The end result was danger to both the children *and* the organization.

Positive Accountability and Disciplinary Policies

As we've discussed, many organizations have historically expressed their employee policies in a negative way. A typical policy might state that an employee "may be disciplined up to and including termination" for "unsatisfactory job performance" which may include "any factors that, in the opinion of the supervisor or manager, are appropriate to determine whether an employee's performance constitutes unsatisfactory job performance." Compare that punitive language with the following "just culture" policy:

> Our Just Culture recognizes the inevitability of human error, does not punish individuals for system failures over which they have no control, and promotes a non-punitive learning environment; however, our Just Culture also holds staff accountable for individual decision-making and actions. To this end, we will balance systemic factors alongside accountability for individual actions to achieve a consistent, fair, and systematic approach to safety.

Which of these two organizations would you rather work in? Which organization do you think is more likely to hear reports of problematic behavior?

In a culture of positive accountability, leaders make it clear that the organization will not punish mere human errors; rather, they will address them with a conversation and with an effort to figure out how to keep the problem from reoccurring. Such mistakes are different from reckless or intentional wrongdoing, which leaders should deal with more seriously.

JUST CULTURE: ERROR, RECKLESSNESS, AND WRONGDOING

The problem with many child protection policies is that they combine what the organization aims for, as an ideal, with what the organization, in its child protection role, cannot tolerate. As a child protection leader, you must promote good practice. At the same time, you must distinguish between human error, recklessness, and wrongdoing. Consider the following scenarios.

Julia is a valued staffer in your day camp program. Your program specifically prohibits staff from "engaging with children outside the camp setting." One camper, Amy, has severe social anxiety. Amy is fond of Julia and often seeks her out when she is feeling overwhelmed amid the daily activities of camp. Amy's parents approach Julia one afternoon and say, "Julia, as you know, Amy has some problems fitting in, but she seems to really connect with you. Would you mind taking some time with her outside camp hours? Maybe going with her to some activities and helping her to engage with other children? We are worried about her social anxiety, but she seems to blossom around you."

Julia, being the good person she is, doesn't think about your child protection policy. After all, it's designed for predators and she is simply helping Amy and her parents. Julia takes Amy to the park; she takes Amy to the zoo; she babysits for Amy while her parents are on a date. And she casually mentions at work that she's done these things. Her supervisor then is in the awkward position of telling Julia that she has just violated the organization's child protection policies.

This is where just culture comes in. In a compliance-driven culture, the supervisor might report to HR a violation of the child protection "code of conduct," resulting in an investigation with pre-determined results. Julia *clearly* violated policy, but how do you deal with the fact that Julia did what she did *in good faith*, not understanding that while her intentions were pure, this is the sort of personal engagement the policies prohibit, and there is a good reason for those policies?

The solution requires separating principles from policies. No harm resulted. Julia was trying to do the right thing for this child and her parents. Therefore, you can treat the violation of the child protection policy as an opportunity to sit down with Julia, explain the reasons behind the policy, and make sure it doesn't happen again. In this situation, leadership should consider the incident as an opportunity for Julia (and the organization) to learn and grow.

Compare that scenario with the following one. Frank is a counselor at a camp that serves youth in foster care with a history of trauma. George is a 14-year-old who struggles with autism spectrum disorder and who has suffered sexual abuse from an uncle. George really loves Frank. He tends to follow Frank around, hugs him constantly, and tells Frank he wants to be his "boyfriend." Frank laughs this off and makes jokes with George. Frank lets George sit on his lap regularly and tousles his hair. Leadership has suggested to Frank that he is out of line, but Frank laughs it off.

Does this situation present differently? Absolutely. Anyone who understands child protection would immediately flag this as a problem. Does it mean that Frank should be fired? That depends. At a minimum, leadership needs to have a significant conversation with Frank regarding his understanding of boundaries and of the effects of sexual trauma on a child or youth. His behavior is at best reckless and should merit significant disciplinary action. If Frank continues to push boundaries, you should treat his behavior as intentional and fire him.

The simplest category is the third: intentional wrongdoing. If you find an employee or volunteer has intentionally abused, neglected, or exploited a child, you not only terminate them but also report them to any appropriate authorities.

Distinguishing between these three categories is vital to your ability to maintain an organizational culture in which employees and volunteers as well as the children and families you support feel cared for and protected. Your policies, procedures and practices must distinguish between (1) human errors that are the result of good intentions, (2) reckless steps that, while well-meaning, deserve a rebuke, and (3) intentional wrongdoing that should result in termination. Unfortunately, few organizations make the effort to ensure they have procedures to make these distinctions.

So, how do we make these distinctions?

I'm so happy you asked! As with all complicated questions, there is no easy answer and it depends. Worksheet #11 may help you work through some of the differences. When determining whether a violation was reckless or intentional, a fundamental issue is whether a reasonable person put in the same situation might make the same decision. Employees who are overwhelmed or under tight deadlines are prone to take shortcuts without thinking of the potential consequences. Employees sometimes make what they believe is the least-worst choice in a situation where they actually have the best interests of the child in mind.

To separate the mistaken decision from the reckless one or the intentional misconduct, consider asking the following questions:

1. Did the employee intend harm?

2. Would a reasonable person have seen the dangers here?

3. Did the employee understand those dangers?

4. Did he or she understand what the policy required, and why, and then willingly choose to do otherwise?

5. Was the employee stuck in a "no-win" bind, such that violating the policy seemed like the least-worst option?

6. Had the employee been counseled about prior violations?

Reckless and intentional violations require the organization to discipline the employee as a means of holding the employee accountable and demonstrating the importance of child protection. After holding the individual accountable, leadership also must determine what happened within the organization's policies, processes, practices, and culture that would allow such behavior.

Creating a strong safety culture in your organization requires more than strong and clear policies. You must also create a culture in which workers feel safe reporting their and their colleagues' errors. Administrators cannot know what is happening in the organization unless front line workers tell them what they see. A just culture is the only way to ensure a transparent and safe program for the youth you serve.

CHAPTER 9

IMPLEMENTING YOUR CHILD PROTECTION POLICY

THE BEST POLICIES in the world won't help you if no one knows about or follows them. In the previous chapter, we discussed the principles of creating a safety culture in your organization. In this chapter, we will discuss how to implement your written policy as a part of that safety culture. There are four pillars to practical implementation: (1) communicating the policies to stakeholders; (2) training people in how the policies apply to their tasks; (3) monitoring compliance with your policies, and (4) responding to violations of policy. Remember that your goal in these child protection policies is to create a culture of safety and healthy accountability in your program. The only way to have that mutual accountability is to ensure clear communication and consistent enforcement.

COMMUNICATING YOUR POLICIES

The first essential component to implementing a strong child protection policy is to plan where, when, and how you will communicate your policies and procedures.

As we explained in Chapter 1, your child protection policy is not a standalone document. Weave it throughout your written communications and agreements with your stakeholders. Be certain that you include relevant rules and procedures in at least five places: (1) your employment or volunteer applications; (2) staff handbooks, (3) minor client handbooks, (4) parent handbooks, and (5) your website. Each of these locations should include only as much information as the intended audience needs. All of them, for example, might include some information about whistleblower protections. Parent handbooks, on the other hand, need an explanation of rules for staff interactions with their children, but they do not need to know the penalties for violating those rules. Public-facing websites don't need detailed information about any of your policies, only a summary proving that child protection is a priority.

In your written documents, communicate reasons for the policies as well as what the rules are. People are much more motivated to follow rules when they understand the "why" as well as the "what." You don't have to include every reason for every audience. Parents and minors, for example, don't need to know that one reason for line-of-sight rules is to avoid false accusations, but you might want to mention the possibility of misunderstandings as well as inappropriate interactions.

TRAINING ABOUT YOUR POLICIES

You can't simply give your workers, parents, and youth copies of your written policies and expect them to follow those rules. We have lost track of the number of times that staff members have testified that, yes, they got a copy of the staff handbook and yes, that is their signature on the statement saying that they would follow it. But they never spent much time reading it and actually have no idea where their copy is now. In fact, as they recall (now that their actions are under review), they can't remember anyone in administration ever mentioning the staff handbook after the initial short discussion. You may be able to enforce a written handbook in terminating an employee, but it won't be enough by itself to defend against claims of maltreatment by a staff member. You must reinforce your policies through periodic training.

What to Include

Be sure that your periodic training includes (1) mandated reporter responsibilities, including recognizing signs and symptoms of abuse, (2) behavior and boundary rules, (3) communications rules, and (4) adult supervision of students. Where you can, put the training into a practical context. For example, rather than simply repeating to your camping staff the rules about communications, also discuss that topic if you encourage your staff to write positive notes during or after the end of your seasonal program.

Whatever training you provide, keep documentation of both the content and who attended. Some organizations keep that material in each worker's individual file, while others keep a separate training notebook. Choose whatever method works best for your organization for both quick retrieval and keeping track of who heard what from you and when.

Whom to Train

You need to train all the staff and volunteers in your program, and you should consider whether to offer training to parents and youth participating in your program. Staff should receive the most training, with volunteers attending as much training as you can get them to fit into their schedules. You usually can require volunteers to attend shorter training sessions, either in person or online, covering the most vital topics such as mandated reporting, boundary rules, and communications rules. You also can limit the training to the contexts where the volunteers will serve. Parents who volunteer to lead an in-program discussion group, for example, don't need to go through the rules for supervising a field trip. Both groups will need to know the signs of maltreatment and their mandated reporting responsibilities, but otherwise they will need to know only what's relevant to their roles.

Similarly, you can offer summary training to parents about what they are most likely to see with their children. They will need to know, for example, that your organization has mandated reporting responsibilities that include reporting any suspicions of abuse or neglect at home. They don't need to know the exact process that your workers must follow. They will need to know your rules on topics such as adult interactions with children, appropriate contact between peers, consequences for bullying, and communications rules. Parents can be your best supervisors of their children and are more likely than anyone to notice when something is wrong. Give them the information that they need and include them in the reporting process.

You may or may not want to include training for children and youth. Some states require boundary training for minors, in which case you have no choice. Many experts are ambivalent about such training because the data is very unclear about whether teaching children increases reporting. The studies that we have indicate that it does not prevent any abuse, mainly because, up to a certain age, children simply are not developmentally capable of objecting to what adults do. The training does result in increased reports of past abuse, however, that can indirectly prevent future abuse.

If you are required to offer the training or decide that it's a good idea for your program, be careful that your training does not make children *responsible* for disclosing abuse. Much well-intended training tries to empower children but ends up making them believe that, if they haven't disclosed abuse, they are somehow responsible when it continues. Be very careful that your training encourages children without making them in any way responsible for telling anyone anything.

When to Train

It's essential that you provide training to workers and stakeholders shortly after they come on board, and then at least annually thereafter. In our experience, it's also helpful to provide training more frequently and in smaller chunks during the year. Periodic lunch-and-learn sessions might be helpful, allowing you to concentrate on a particular aspect of your policy or invite a guest speaker. Some organizations have periodic newsletters that include a section on policy. Hypothetical situations and scenarios are much more memorable than recitations of policy, so find ways to apply the rules in real life. Tabletop exercises sometimes work for shorter meetings. Sending periodic emails with a lesson learned from a news article can be extremely helpful. A combination of yearly in-depth training with frequent reminders during the rest of the year might be the best way for your program to make its rules a strong part of your organizational culture.

MONITORING AND SUPERVISION

The next foundation stone of a strong child protection policy is knowing whether people are actually following it. There are only two ways for administrators to know what is happening in their organizations. The first is for administrators themselves to see behavior, and the second is for front-line staff to tell you what they are seeing. To get those reports, you must establish avenues of communication and clearly communicate that your organization takes reports seriously and protects people who report concerns.

Your organization must have a procedure for everyone to monitor interactions, both adult-youth and youth-youth inter-changes. As you develop your policies and practices, take a long look at the following principles:

Don't be hyper-vigilant. One of the fastest ways to torpedo employee morale is to micromanage and overanalyze all their actions. Similarly, we are seeing more research showing that constantly supervised minors tend to have higher levels of anxiety and depression, perhaps because they never learn to navigate conflict on their own. In the long run, treating adults and youth as though you don't trust them to make good decisions will harm them and, by extension, your organization.

The ability to protect children is best based on trusting and healthy relationships among your staff, volunteers and youth. You must monitor interactions to prevent or catch inappropriate behavior; you also must find the balance that creates a positive and trusting environment that can best protect the youth in your care.

Keep all risks in mind. As we've discussed earlier, it's easy to get so focused on screening out pedophiles that we forget other common risks, such as youth-on-youth bullying. We also should recognize that some staff members who cross the lines aren't classic pedophiles, but ordinary people who drift into inappropriate relationships with older teens or overly sexualized youth. The screening you do for predators may not catch those situations; the best defense against these people is consistent monitoring and enforcement of boundary guidelines.

Pay close attention to high-risk areas. When you are developing or reviewing your policies, pay attention to the high-risk situations in your program. You may learn these from incident reports, or you may be able to just ask the youth and staff what areas they see as problematic. Youth in your program usually know the secluded areas where bullying happens; be sure that you know those areas as well. Other situations where youth may be vulnerable are travel, particularly overnight trips, and public events. Pay particular attention to these areas when writing your policies and in your yearly audits.

If you can't prohibit one-on-one contact, then be sure you have specific rules for those times that you allow the contact.

Line-of-sight rules and visibility requirements will be particularly important here.

Empower your workers. Be sure that your staff and volunteers know that they are an important line of defense in monitoring interactions. An important part of this communication is a clear whistleblower protection policy, as we outline in the next section. Also be sure that you encourage mutual accountability in emails, newsletters, and every informal communication that you can. Understand and help your workers understand that you aren't creating a tattletale culture, but one of mutually encouraging and reminding each other of important safety rules.

Catch people doing the right thing. In this area, as in all areas of a strong child protection policy, positive reinforcement works better than negative. When you see or learn of appropriate behavior, acknowledge and reward it. Ask your workers to tell you about the positive examples they see. Encouraging them to report positive interactions as well as violations will help build the culture of trust that you need for strong child protection.

Document reports and observations. As with all areas where someone can make a claim, document your observations and any reports that you get. This principle applies to positive interactions as well as problems. Your written records should provide as clear and complete a picture as possible of how your organization functions. When you do your yearly audits, you need to be able to rely on incident reports and employee files to know what policies are working for your program and what problem areas you need to work on.

Enforce your protocol. We discuss various principles for responding to policy violations in the next section of this chapter. For now, we will just reinforce the importance of consistent, even-handed enforcement of your rules. If you model corner-cutting, then your workers will learn that lesson from you and do the same thing.

DO YOU WANT CAMERAS?

One common question we hear is whether good supervision requires surveillance cameras. In our experience, camera systems don't directly prevent maltreatment; they merely document it so that you can respond. If you are thinking about cameras or already have them, be sure to think through the following common issues:

How long can you preserve the video? Sometimes you don't get reports of maltreatment until well after the fact. At the same time, storing video files can be expensive. Know whether your budget will stretch to keeping the video long enough to be worthwhile and as long as the rules and custom in your area require. Also, be sure that your document retention policy includes video, and that you consistently follow that policy. The last thing you want is for someone to claim that you deliberately lost video of a particular incident.

Can you account for blind spots? Every camera has blind spots. In fact, for restrooms, changing rooms, and other areas that require privacy, you cannot have camera coverage. Even in a public place, the camera will not cover the entire area. So, decide ahead of time how you will supervise those areas. Cameras are never an adequate substitute for in-person observations.

Do you have enough personnel to review the footage? Just having the video won't do anything to prevent inappropriate interactions. If you want to use cameras for proactive child protection, as opposed to just passive evidence collection, you must spend time reviewing the footage. It's impossible to review all of it, but you need to at least have someone responsible for random spot reviews. The cameras literally are just another set of eyes, only they don't spontaneously report anything. If you want to keep the cameras just to check out claims of maltreatment, then the spot reviews are not as important, but your document retention time becomes a bigger factor. Decide how you plan to use the cameras and develop appropriate rules.

Do you have a policy about parent review and retention? If you have cameras, parents inevitably will ask to review the footage. Develop a policy based on your state's laws and privacy rules. In jurisdictions without specific laws, we usually recommend allowing parents to view the video to avoid claims of a cover-up. Whether you have to blur the other minors' faces first depends on your local laws and rules. In most jurisdictions, you won't have to do that blurring just for viewing because the parents are only seeing what they could see if they were in the area at the time.

However, we strongly recommend that you never allow the parents to record what they are viewing or otherwise provide them with a separate copy. Putting that video out in the wild definitely invades the privacy interests of all the other people, particularly the minors, in the video. You need to do everything in your power to protect that information.

WHISTLEBLOWER POLICIES

An important part of effective monitoring is listening to the people who are most likely to observe any policy violations. One common pattern we see when defending claims against youth organizations is that administrators always insist that no one knew about the accused worker's violation of policies or predatory tendencies. Then, when we start interviewing other staff, it turns out that many people saw many red flags. But they either didn't think anyone would believe them or feared retaliation, so they never said anything. Thus, the administrators who could have stopped the abuse never knew about any of the problematic behavior. If you want to know about red flags, you must have a robust policy that protects whistleblowers who see and report those red flags.

Many states and localities have strong whistleblower statutes. If your organization is located in one of those jurisdictions, those requirements must be part of your policy. If you aren't subject to such laws or want to include protections beyond the required ones, be certain that you consider each of the following areas:

Protections for whistleblowers. You need very clear statements that people who make good faith reports of violations will be protected and that your organization does not allow retaliation against them. This is one area where you can make the language as strong as you want. Your workers, parents, and clients need to know that you will take their concerns seriously.

We don't recommend that you make any promises about believing reports. As we discuss in Chapter 10, the best investigations are objective and don't start with any presumptions about what the facts will show. Both the accuser and the accused need to believe that you will be impartial and not start with any bias one way or the other. What you can, and should, promise is to *listen* to all reports, take them seriously, and investigate them thoroughly.

Give feedback to those who report violations. Be sure that you respond to the person who made the report. Nothing will sap morale faster than having people within your organization think that their reports go into a black hole where nothing happens. Privacy issues may prevent you from sharing too much information about how you handled the report. However, you should at least (a) acknowledge the report, (b) thank the reporter, and (c) provide updates where you can about how the report is proceeding through the system.

Accountability for everyone. Ensure that your procedure has a way to report anyone who works with your organization. If reports about staff and students go to your Assistant Director, for example, who receives reports about that Assistant Director? If someone has concerns about administrators, is there someone outside the administration to whom they can report their concerns? Consider each person who works with your organization, all the way up to and including Board members, and have an avenue for anyone else to report concerns. Know who is accountable to whom and who will investigate concerns about each position in your program.

Be transparent about your policy. Clearly set out your whistleblower protections and procedure in your various handbooks. You might find it helpful to put a strong statement about whistleblower protections in your governing documents or in communications from your Board to staff and stakeholders. Beyond that, consider posting at least a summary on your website and in public-facing documents. Finding multiple avenues to emphasize the importance that you place on reports of policy violations will help encourage people to let you know if they see problematic behavior.

A credible whistleblower policy is an essential foundation stone for your child protection policy. You want to know about problematic behavior as early as possible, and the only people who can tell you are your front-line workers, parents, and students. Be certain that you have a transparent and clear avenue for them to report, and that they believe that you will protect them when they do so.

RESPONDING TO CONCERNS AND VIOLATIONS

The final building block to implementing your policy is to respond appropriately to the reports that you receive. The true test of your organization's child protection policies and practices is how it responds to reports and holds violators accountable. You need a method for ensuring reports get to the right person, that you triage them appropriately, and that you respond to them in a way that builds a transparent culture among your staff. Your system should (1) create tiers of reports and responses depending on the severity of the issue; (2) ensure a measured reaction based on the severity of reports; and (3) demonstrate transparency in reporting results.

TIERS OF REPORTS

Picking the right route for reporting is critical to how you will manage it, and the reporting pathways your organization chooses will significantly affect your organization's culture and outcomes. How you structure reporting depends on a number of considerations, including the size of your organization and the different departments and locations you have.

We once were privy to a child protection summary from a youth-serving organization that has offices in many different places. The summary gave the number of child protection incidents reported in each location where the organization works. Here's a fictionalized version of the actual chart we received:

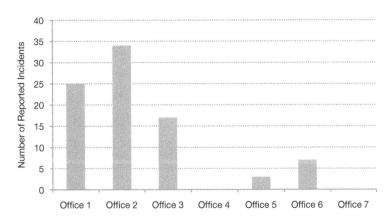

Reported Incidents by Office During the Year

Now think about how different people might interpret this information. The CEO and the Child Safety Team might think that Office 2 has a serious child protection problem and that Offices 4 and 7 are doing great. Donors to your organization might think you have a problem keeping beneficiaries safe.

After digging deeper, the organization realized that this chart summarized *all reports* involving child protection issues received from each office. What we found was that Offices 1 and 2, for example, had a robust child protection team and reported anything that arose that might impact child protection. Other offices—4 and 7—didn't yet have a full child protection team and received no reports. The number of reports told us very little about the level of child safety in each program.

It's very important, then, to ensure that your organization classifies reports appropriately. Using a "just culture" approach, here are some categories into which you might classify them: (1) Concerns; (2) Risky behavior or policy violations not resulting in harm; (3) Unintentional policy violations resulting in harm (human error); and (4) Reckless or intentional policy violations, resulting in harm. Worksheet #13 provides a flow chart that you can review and adapt as you consider the following discussion of those categories.

Concerns

Sometimes an employee, volunteer, or community member simply has concerns about how the organization is implementing its child protection policies. Perhaps they have a recommendation for improving policy or general worries about how the policies are working in practice. Whenever a true accident occurs, the organization should treat that incident as an opportunity to review how changes to child protection policy and practice might prevent such accidents in the future.

Risky Behavior and/or Policy Violations (Resulting in No Injury or Harm)

Humans inevitably engage in risky behavior. Serving youth itself carries risks and requires trade-offs between the benefits of helping children develop into responsible adults and protecting them from the dangers of the world. So, it's not surprising to see even staff of very safety-conscious organizations violate their own policies. It may be a question of compliance fatigue, or a situation of too much to do, too little time to get it all done, or a decision to ignore a safety policy that seems to get in the way of meeting the needs of the youth. When you see these risky behaviors or hear reports that staff are not following policy, consider it an opportunity to improve your child safety practice and promote a healthy organizational culture at the same time.

In a healthy organization with good "just culture" practices, this type of report (along with reports of concerns) should constitute the majority of those you receive. In fact, if you are *not* receiving regular reports from front-line staff regarding general concerns about child safety or concerns about whether the policies are being followed, that lack of reporting may be an indication that your team needs a refresher training and a reminder of the importance of monitoring child safety.

A significant question for youth-serving organizations is whether reports of general concerns, "risky" behavior, and unintentional policy violations should go through the same reporting channels as those used for reporting situations in which an employee has acted intentionally or recklessly, or in which a child has suffered harm. Our recommendation, following "just culture" concepts, is that these matters be handled in a less formal matter.

If the same members of your team who investigate serious misconduct are also those reviewing and responding to less serious child protection policy and practice concerns, the unintended effect may be to create fear among your team members when those personnel show up for what should be an informal, engaging, and positive review.

Unintentional Policy Violations Resulting in Harm

Humans err, and although these errors won't affect the children and youth we serve most of the time, sometimes they do. These reports need to be handled with more sensitivity and greater attention. Organizations have a duty to keep children safe, and a failure to do so could expose the organization to liability for negligence. It's important to understand what happened, and why. It's also critical to ensure the child, youth, or other individual harmed is helped to recover. The more difficult question is whether and how to discipline the worker who made the error. You simply must gauge each situation individually and make the most just decision that you can.

Reckless or Intentional Policy Violations

Allegations that an employee has recklessly or intentionally violated your child protection policy require a more formal response and accountability and may require significant disciplinary measures. Organizations must recognize, however, that before we label a violation as reckless or intentional, we first must understand the *motivation* behind the action. "Intentional" here means violating the policy for one's own benefit in disregard of a significant harm.

"Reckless," likewise, means acting with a conscious disregard for the fact that there is a high risk of a negative result.

ASSIGNING DIFFERENT TYPES OF REPORTS FOR A RESPONSE

When a report comes in, someone in your organization needs to give it at least a preliminary classification. We recommend the Child Safety Coordinator, working with the Child Safety Team, serve this function or create a team that can triage and direct reports about child protection policies. The CSC can then make sure the most appropriate personnel handle the report. Worksheet #14 is a flow chart that you can review and adapt as you develop your response protocols.

For concerns, "risky behavior," and policy violations that do not result in harm, the approach should be one focused more on systemic quality improvement and less on individual actions. Such an approach should:

Use positive language. Instead of referring to "reports of child safety concerns" or "incidents," discuss the referral in terms of an opportunity to improve safety for the team as well as those it serves. Instead of "investigation," use terms such as "policy and practice review."

Reward self-reporting. In a study of surgeons, providing financial incentives for physicians to report surgical complications significantly increased their self-reporting. Other organizations have employees sign a "values pledge" that affirms the importance of reporting errors. The key is to ensure that reporting of concerns and policy violations resulting in no harm is seen as a helpful part of your organization's child abuse prevention efforts.

Involve frank and transparent conversations. Responding to these types of reports requires the ability to have frank, sometimes difficult, conversations with staff without creating defensiveness. While the approach is a "softer" one, employees need to understand that abuse prevention is important to the organization.

A more difficult scenario involves human errors that do result in harm. Consider, for example, a group home that requires that staff supervise youth at all times. During a field trip to a water park, a staff member has to seek medical attention for a child who has fallen and cut her head. While she takes that child to the first-aid center, two other young teens sneak off. Later, one of the teens says the other teen groped her inappropriately.

Responding to such situations may require a dual approach. One track addresses the human error element in an empathetic but firm manner. The other track activates the incident response team to address the needs of the victim, legal requirements for reporting to authorities, potential liabilities, and potential harm to the organization's reputation.

For each of these types of reports, your Child Safety Coordinator might be the best person to respond to the employee or team that is the subject of the concern or that is accused of the policy violation. He or she can proceed using an informal corrective process focused on improving overall child safety rather than on the actions of one or two individuals. Through this systemic approach, he or she can build a reputation among staff as a source of support, information, and encouragement.

The final category is reckless and intentional policy violations (misconduct), with or without resulting harm. These reports demand a firm response, whether or not they have resulted in harm. First, of course, a preliminary screening should be done to determine whether the conduct was truly reckless or intentional, as noted above. If you determine that the violation falls in either category, we recommend that these allegations be treated as formal investigations and conducted by individuals trained to do so. While the Child Safety Coordinator may be the person in charge of assigning the case, the Incident Response Team should take the lead on investigating such issues.

ANONYMOUS REPORTS

How will your organization handle anonymous reports? Allowing anonymous reports may promote reporting, as it is a means of protecting the privacy of those who have information about abuse but are afraid of repercussions and reprisals. On the other hand, accepting anonymous reporting allows disgruntled individuals to weaponize the system to make false allegations. Such reports also may be missing important details, but offer no opportunity for follow-up to get more facts. If your organization accepts anonymous reports, be sure that you treat those alleging reckless or intentional misconduct as seriously as those coming from identified sources and develop ways to investigate the claims.

As the flow chart in Worksheet #14 shows, when faced with either a negative outcome or a reported policy violation, those responsible for care quality and employee discipline must go through a decision-making process when determining how to address the issue. In most cases, the investigation of the incident involves much more than simply determining the facts. Questions focus on *why* the incident occurred. What were the systemic factors? What was going on with the employee? Was the training adequate? The implementation of the policy? The monitoring? Contrast such an approach with that too often taken by many managers, who are concerned primarily with determining which individual failed to meet expectations and then determining the proper discipline.

This chapter has only scratched the surface of the principles of communication and supervision in the workplace. Both are areas covered by multitudes of experts and general principles. We have discussed, however, factors that are uniquely important to solid child protection policies. Be certain that you consider and decide how best to incorporate these principles into your program to be sure that everyone in your program both understands and is following your child safety protocols.

WORKSHEET #11

Discipline for Policy Violations

As you think about how to hold employees accountable for policy violations, you should "game" the outcomes of various scenarios. This works best when conducted as a tabletop exercise with a diverse team from different levels and functions within the organization. While violations are often unique, the following questions may help as you consider various scenarios.

1. What is the pathway for employees, volunteers, children/youth, and parents to make complaints when they feel that someone affiliated with the organization (which could include a child or youth participant) is doing something wrong or risky? Is that pathway well-known? How often is it used?

_____

_____

_____

_____

2. When a complaint about wrong or risky behavior not involving an actual incident of harm is made, who responds? What is the current process?

_____

_____

_____

_____

3. With the current process, what efforts are made to "triage" the issue to determine whether there are systemic issues that contributed and/or whether the violation occurred due to human error vs. reckless or intentional behavior?

_____

_____

_____

_____

4. What sort of discipline and accountability is meted out for policy violations that were not intentional or reckless and do not result in harm to a child?

_____

_____

_____

_____

5. Is there a process in place for working with those who committed or contributed to unintentional or human error policy violations to devise solutions so the mistake won't be repeated? If so, how are those solutions conveyed to the rest of the team?

_____

_____

_____

_____

WORKSHEET #12

Report Triage Form

Date: _____

Location: _____

Reported to: _____

☐ Anonymous Report

☐ Self-Report

☐ Third-Party Report

Summary of Report:

_____

_____

_____

_____

Preliminary Classification:

☐ **Concern**: Reporter expresses a concern regarding the impact of or efficacy of a child protection policy, practice, or process; recommends improvements or review.

☐ **Policy Violation**: Reporter expresses a specific or general lack of compliance with child protection policy, no specific incident of harm to a child.

☐ **Incident Involving Error/Policy Violation**. Child has suffered the following harm:

_____ and the

following policy may have been violated: _____

_____.

☐ **Reckless/Intentional Behavior**

Policy involved: _____

Prior incidents? _____

Harm resulting? _____

Assigned to:

☐ Human Resources: _____

☐ Incident Response Team: _____

☐ Child Protection Lead: _____

WORKSHEET #13

Note: Track assignment can change, depending on the facts.

Concern	Risky Behavior or Policy Violation	Unintentional Harm	Recklessness or Misconduct
▪ Informal review ▪ Reward reporting ▪ Address concerns ▪ Use as example ▪ Demonstrate quality improvement process ▪ Show results of how policy and practice is improved	▪ Informal review ▪ Reward reporting ▪ Address violation ▪ Explain why behavior is risky ▪ Maintain confidentiality ▪ Use feedback for quality improvement ▪ Show results	▪ Formal investigation ▪ For employees, address violation ▪ For victims, treatment and care ▪ Audit policies and practices for systemic issues ▪ Address legal requirements	▪ Formal investigation ▪ Public accountability ▪ Empathy for victim(s) ▪ Audit and root cause analysis ▪ Differentiate the "why" for staff ▪ Reinforce early reporting

CHAPTER 10
RESPONDING TO SERIOUS INCIDENTS

ET'S ACKNOWLEDGE A few facts about lawyers. When our clients face a crisis, our lawyer's instincts prompt us to admit nothing, deny everything, and stall for time while we figure out our best defense. Unfortunately, this time also is the only opportunity that you will have to be transparent and shape the narrative about what happened.

Your goals in a crisis are much broader than simply avoiding legal liability. You also must care for employees, youth and their families. Youth-serving organizations often think in terms of sacrifice for the greater good of caring for vulnerable people. That self-sacrifice and caring does not require corporate suicide—going out of business would violate your organization's obligation to current staff and future clients. Meeting your larger mission when confronted with a serious abuse allegation requires transparency and accepting responsibility early.

Sometimes your responsibilities to balance your obligations to your organization and your employees, youth and families will seem to conflict. Fortunately, early transparency is not always incompatible with a vigorous defense of a later lawsuit. Some tasks will take priority at different points in time, and you may need to find creative ways of meeting both goals. This chapter will show you some ways to balance your mission and your organizational duty of self-preservation.

PREPARE AHEAD OF TIME

Don't wait until you have a serious incident to start planning for it. There are several important things that the Incident Response Team should start doing right away to be sure that your organization can handle a serious incident or major crisis.

MANDATED REPORTING

A critical step in your response to any incident is to quickly determine whether you are required to report the incident to outside authorities. Do the groundwork now to research the rules and train your workers (including volunteers). As we mentioned in the chapter on training, also consider whether parents in your program could benefit from knowing these rules and procedures.

In general, there are two types of mandated reports. The most common is the requirement to report suspected child abuse to either law enforcement or child protective services (CPS) authorities. The other is to report incidents of injury or abuse to licensing and regulatory authorities. In this chapter, we'll discuss the responsibilities that your organization may have.

WHO, WHAT, WHEN, WHERE, AND HOW

Let's first discuss the legal responsibilities that an individual or organization may have to report suspected incidents of child abuse. When a report of suspected child abuse is required by law, failure to make it can result in criminal liability for the person who failed to make the report. In our experience, law enforcement has recently taken a more aggressive stance and brought criminal charges against individuals for failing to report child abuse. In some jurisdictions, failing to report child abuse is itself deemed a type of child abuse.

Who's a Mandated Reporter?

If your organization works with minors, then in the vast majority of U.S. jurisdictions, all of your workers are mandated reporters. Your incident response team should ensure it fully understands the child abuse reporting requirements for each jurisdiction in which your organization operates.

Jurisdictions that require individuals to report child abuse also generally provide immunity for reports made in "good faith." That same immunity extends to reports made in good faith by individuals who are not mandated by law to report but who do so voluntarily. Because those who report in good faith have immunity from liability for reporting, we recommend that you instruct all staff and volunteers to report, whether they are specifically covered by the statute's requirements or not. At the same time, as we discuss in the section about insurance, because it's easy for someone to allege a bad faith motive, be sure that your insurance covers any potential claims.

What Needs to be Reported and When?

Each jurisdiction—state, territory, or nation—will have different requirements as to what triggers a child maltreatment reporting duty. These requirements may differ in three key aspects: (1) what constitutes "abuse"; (2) what constitutes "reasonable grounds to report"; and (3) when the report must be made.

"Child abuse" is defined by statute and involves (1) a child, as local law defines a minor; and (2) suspected maltreatment, which generally includes the following categories:

Physical abuse, or any intentional infliction of physical harm to a child. In some jurisdictions, there is an exception for corporal punishment inflicted by a parent or adult caregiver. Hazing or physical abuse inflicted by other children may constitute physical abuse.

Emotional abuse, usually defined as intentional behavior that causes significant harm to a child's emotional development or sense of self-worth. It may be active—for example, threats or intimidation—or passive, as when a parent rejects a child or withholds needed love and support. In some jurisdictions, allowing a child to witness domestic violence is deemed to be emotional abuse. In others, bullying by other children could be classified as emotional abuse.

Sexual abuse and sexual exploitation, including any kind of improper exposure of the child to sexual content or activity. A frequent issue that arises involves child-on-child sexual contact. Often the law includes an exception for sexual contact between young adolescents who are close in age. A surprising number of jurisdictions include voluntary "sexting" (sending nude selfies) to other minors in the definition of sexual exploitation, requiring a report to authorities.

Neglect, or the failure to provide a child with the basic necessities and support he or she needs. The most common type of child maltreatment, neglect may involve educational neglect or failing to follow compulsory education requirements; failure to provide adequate food, clothing, and shelter, or failure to provide necessary medical care, with some exceptions for religious objections.

Having "reasonable grounds" or "reasonable suspicion" that child abuse is occurring or has occurred is what generally triggers an individual's duty to report. As one court noted, "the requirement of a reasonable belief as a prerequisite is a low standard," one that mandates a report "if there are any facts from which one could reasonably conclude that a child had been abused.'"

When does one report? Depending on the state, you must report "immediately," "as soon as possible," or "within 24 hours" after the reporter has grounds for concern.

Where is the Report Made and To Whom?

In most jurisdictions, a mandated report goes to the child protective services agency, although some areas require notification to law enforcement. Each organization should know the local reporting requirements as well as how reports should be communicated.

How Should Our Organization Make the Report?

Depending on the local law, making the mandated report may be the personal responsibility of the individual with grounds to believe the abuse has occurred. In practice, many organizations have a centralized process in which the individual who seeks to make the report does so through a designated person such as the Child Safety Coordinator or a leader on the Incident Response Team. Our recommendation is that, unless your statute prohibits internal reporting, the worker inform the CSC or someone on the IRT and then the CSC/IRT and the worker make that report together. That way, the worker has fulfilled his or her obligation, and the organization is not surprised by an investigation. More importantly, the CSC/IRT can add any important context or previous incidents that are suspicious only in hindsight.

Exceptions

To preserve confidentiality, some mandated reporter laws excuse certain professions from reporting suspected child abuse in limited situations. In many states, for example, a priest or other member of the clergy is not required to report suspected abuse that he or she learns of in the course of providing spiritual counseling. This privilege, however, applies only when the clergy member is engaged in the specific provision of spiritual counseling, such as may occur in the confessional. More recently, it appears legislators are revoking this exception and are requiring clergy to report suspected child abuse. If your organization is used to a particular exception, be sure that your IRT researches the current legal parameters—don't assume anything.

REPORTING TO LICENSING AND REGULATORY AGENCIES

In addition to legal requirements to report to child protection or law enforcement, your organization may need to report maltreatment or accidents to regulatory agencies. Common examples of requirements to report to the licensing agency include incidents where a child is injured and requires medical attention other than first aid; any situation in which a child becomes lost or is left alone; or any emergency requiring children to be relocated. Regulations often require that if a program reports suspected child abuse to authorities—even if it did not occur on-site—the program must make a duplicate report to the licensing agency. Also ensure that you understand the deadlines for making required reports—these are often "immediately" or "within 24 hours."

Make Reporting Easy on Your Staff

Because mandated and required reporting can be so complicated, we recommend you create a simple decision tree for your staff, such as the one in Worksheet #15. Such a decision tree would be a great project for your Incident Response Team to work on with legal counsel.

INSURANCE POLICIES

In the insurance coverage audit, have your insurance expert confirm that the insurance covers child maltreatment, including sexual molestation. The other critical issue is to ensure that you understand which policies cover which claims for which time period. As an increasing number of jurisdictions have moved to eliminate statutes of limitation (time limits) for bringing child sexual assault, molestation, and exploitation claims, you may find your organization exposed to liability for an incident that occurred many years ago.

Even if your jurisdiction has not yet eliminated the time bar to bringing a claim, it may do so in the future. To ensure that you're ready, you will need to ensure that you have a file available that indicates each type of insurance coverage your organization has held, the time periods covered, and the contact information for making a claim. Because insurers often merge or change names, you may have some research to do if you work for an organization with a long history of service. If your organization is large enough, consider hiring researchers who specialize in locating these policies.

For both your current and past policies, review them and ask:

1. Is this a "claims made" or "occurrence" policy? In other words, does it cover claims made now, or claims regarding an incident that occurred during a certain time period?

2. Do I have "tail" insurance that covers claims for events that occurred prior to my current policy becoming effective?

3. Have I considered all the risks—injury, abuse, harassment, exploitation—to those I serve—staff, children, volunteers, and community members—and does my insurance cover those risks and potential claimants?

We recommend also that child and youth-serving organizations carry defamation insurance because some organizations have found themselves accused of false or bad faith reports to child protection authorities. Most states provide absolute immunity for good faith reports, but even in those states, a plaintiff can allege bad faith reasons for making a report. For both child maltreatment and defamation, have your insurance expert ensure that your coverage at least covers the costs of an attorney (or team of attorneys) to defend your organization in any litigation.

DOCUMENT RETENTION

Your organization must have a document retention policy. How that looks depends very much on the laws and policies of your jurisdiction, what similarly situated organizations are doing, what your licensing or regulatory authorities require, and how long your exposure to a lawsuit may be.

You should retain some documents permanently. The National Council of Nonprofits, for example, recommends retaining the following documents permanently:

- Articles of Incorporation
- Audit reports, from independent audits
- Corporate resolutions
- Checks
- Determination Letter from the IRS, and correspondence relating to it
- Financial statements (year-end)
- Insurance policies
- Minutes of board meetings and annual meetings of members
- Real estate deeds, mortgages, bills of sale
- Tax returns

These, of course, are financial documents. What you may be more concerned about are those documents related to potential claims that an employee, volunteer, or other person connected with your organization has abused or exploited a child or youth under your care.

In such an event, the issues to think about are the following:

What is the statute of limitations for claims against your organization? As many states are moving toward eliminating time-bars to claims of abuse and exploitation, we now believe you should keep permanently at least the following documents: (1) personnel files of any individual who has been accused of abuse against a child or youth in your program; (2) records of any allegations of abuse against a child or youth in your program, including any documentation and results of an investigation; and (3) relevant documents for the time period of those claims such as employee rosters, time sheets, program schedules, and youth attendance sheets.

What do government agencies recommend? A quick internet search for "document retention policies" will give you a good idea of what different federal and state agencies recommend regarding retention of different categories of documents. If it's "good enough for government work," it's probably good enough for you.

The key here is not to prescribe for your organization any specific document retention policy. Rather, what you need to keep in mind is how you are going to answer the question in the future, "Why don't you have this particular document?" If you create a reasonable policy in line with industry standards and *consistently follow that policy*, you'll be fine. It's deviations from the policy that get organizations in trouble once lawyers get involved.

COMMUNICATIONS POLICIES

The final area you can work on ahead of time is planning your communications in the event of a serious injury or allegation. The last thing you want is for your staff to defend themselves on social media. The next-to-the-last thing you want is to have the news media show an administrator peering fearfully around a door saying, "No comment." Be sure that your staff policies include clear directions about who is authorized to talk to the media, parents, and stakeholders. Also plan how you will communicate a crisis to your staff. They should not learn about it from third parties.

In your planning process, consider creating templates for public statements and letters or emails to parents. Even if you have to leave a lot of blanks to be filled in later, having somewhere to start will be better than staring at a blank page. Work with a person experienced in public relations who can help you with a formula for those statements.

WHEN BAD THINGS HAPPEN (TO GOOD ORGANIZATIONS)

It's a Friday evening, and the director has just gotten home from a long week of running a summer day camp. She has two days to get ready for the next week-long session with a new group of campers. The phone rings, and it's the mother of a college student who has been working in the program during his summer break. He's just been arrested on child molestation charges and is being held without bond at the county jail. His mother says a parent of a second grader in one of the past sessions apparently reported the young man *"touched my bottom when I was in the bathroom and hurt me."*

If you are that director, this is the section of the book, including Worksheet #16, that you pull out. Whenever you have a serious incident, whether an accident or allegation of abuse, you and your organization's Incident Response Team need to take swift, serious action. We've discussed in prior chapters how you build that team so that it is prepared to respond to a significant crisis resulting from an incident in which serious allegations of abuse have been leveled. Of course, you don't want to find yourself in a situation where you're activating that team for the first time following a crisis. So, in this section we will walk you through the steps your IRT will need to prepare for and carry out in case of an emergency. Worksheet #16 provides a summary checklist to help you stay on track.

It's not uncommon for an organization to learn of a serious incident third hand. Police and child protective services may already be involved. Parents may already have heard about the incident. In some situations, the next call may be from local media outlets wanting to know what happened and what your organization intends to do about it. You need to activate your IRT quickly and let its members start responding.

The timeline we've included in Worksheet #16 discusses how your response should play out in the short- and longer-term. Here, we're going to focus on what your IRT should do the moment you receive the accusation.

YOUR FIRST RESPONSES

Isolate the accused. As soon as you're informed of an allegation that a member of your staff, a volunteer, a contractor, or another minor has committed abuse against a youth, your first responsibility is to isolate that individual from interacting with the alleged victim as well as other children and youth your organization serves. Remove him or her from your physical facilities and cut off access to email and any other program resources. Doing so does not mean you necessarily believe the allegations, nor is this isolation a form of punishment. Rather, doing so (1) protects the accused from allegations that he or she has continued any abuse; (2) demonstrates the seriousness of the allegations; and (3) provides an environment for a proper investigation. If the allegation involves someone on your program's payroll, whether to suspend the accused with or without pay is purely a budgetary decision, as long as you are following a consistent and established policy.

The designated employee-accused contact on your incident response team should meet with the accused and explain to them the allegations and the interim action the organization will take. This person should *not* interview or take statements from the accused. Ensure that, at least temporarily, you limit the accused's access to the organization's computer system, obtain any keys and equipment, such as cell phones or laptops, that the employee may have, and provide a method to return to the employee any personal items he or she may have left on your campus—unless, of course, those items may be considered evidence in the matter.

In our scenario above, where the accused has been arrested, isolating him from your program may not be an issue. How you communicate with him, however, will be. Before you ever are faced with such a crisis, have your IRT work through the following questions:

1. How do we maintain an appropriate distance from the accused employee without prejudging the accusations? Should we hire counsel for the employee? Some organizations find that ensuring the employee has an attorney both protects the employee and the organization. Some insurance companies offer that extra coverage for an additional premium.

2. Who should make contact with the accused, and how? If the employee has been arrested and is in jail, phone communications between your staff and the employee may be recorded and subject to public disclosure. And anything the employee says to someone (other than perhaps his pastor, spouse, or attorney) is not protected.

3. Is there a specific script you should follow or a sample letter you should write in advance for these situations? It's better to plan such a response ahead of time rather than wait until the crisis is upon you.

Make mandated or required reports and notify your insurer. Ensure that you've reported the incident to the appropriate authorities in a timely manner, as we discussed earlier in this chapter, according to the policy that we hope your IRT has already established. At the same time, notify your current insurance carrier and, in situations of historical abuse, the insurer whose policy covers that time period. Remember that many states and jurisdictions have extended or eliminated statutes of limitation for child sexual abuse and exploitation accusations, in which case you may find yourself facing a claim from decades past.

Conduct a brief survey of witnesses and gather necessary documents. While you may not be able to completely determine what happened within the first 24 hours or so, you should at least gather documentation that relates to the incident and have the attorney on your IRT interview any witnesses to the incident, to the extent possible. Interviewing the accused is a different matter that should be handled carefully in collaboration with your attorney and any attorney for the employee.

At this stage, you aren't seeking a full investigation of the incident. But you should take the following actions, at a minimum:

1. Secure the employee/accused's personnel file, including any background check information, time sheets, and work history.

2. Identify and take written statements from any employees, volunteers, or other adults who may have been in the vicinity of the incident around the time it is alleged to have occurred.

3. If your facility has cameras, secure any video recordings that may have captured the area where the incident occurred on the day or days in question.

4. Secure the files containing any information the organization has on the alleged victim.

Plan meetings with employees, parents, and stakeholders; prepare statements. In our scenario above, it's likely that even if your other employees, parents, board members, volunteers, donors, and members of your community don't already know about the arrest and allegations, they soon will. Each of these groups will have different levels of concern, and you need to have plans in place to determine how you would address the concerns of each. Our general advice is that the closer the concerned individual is to your program, the more that person needs to know.

At the same time, there are certain things that must remain confidential for the protection of the alleged victim and his or her family, due to legal requirements, and to maintain a clean, independent investigation. Your IRT should think through how it would handle discussions with each of the following groups:

Parents of other children and youth in the program will be concerned that their children are unsafe. In the case of alleged sexual abuse of a child, they may question whether their child was a victim. They may also fear the emotional impact on their child of the allegations. For these parents, you should explain the allegations that have been made and explain how you (and law enforcement or other agencies) are responding to them. Express that, while you can't provide certain details due to legal protections, you are very concerned about the victim and are working to find out what happened and why. If possible, provide these parents with resources to help them and their children deal with the grief, anxiety, and worry that serious abuse incidents naturally cause for everyone in a community. These resources might include contact information for local child advocacy centers or a list of trauma-informed therapists in the area. Many of our clients have a counselor present at a parent meeting to help parents understand how to talk to their children about the incident, what behavior to expect, and where to find more help.

Employees, key volunteers, and Board members need to be kept aware of the progress of the investigation and assured that the organization is seeking to determine what happened, to ensure accountability for any wrongdoing, and to improve the organization's ability to serve and protect those it serves as well as its own staff. For this group, explain how the investigation will be carried out and what employees can expect. Will law enforcement, licensing authority personnel, or child protection agents be asking questions? How long will the investigation take? What should they say or not say among themselves or to friends and family regarding the situation?

Media and the community need to understand that whatever has happened, your organization cares about the children and families it serves, that you are concerned about the victim and his or her family, and that you will be as transparent as possible about the investigation and outcome as you are able given legal privacy and confidentiality requirements.

The key in your communications with each of these important constituencies is to demonstrate the values that have made your organization a safe, trusted provider of services to children and youth. These values likely include discretion and respect for privacy, transparency, accountability, and empathy. Conveying these values in the face of a crisis will be difficult. That's why it's important *now* to have your IRT draft scripts or templates that you can adjust depending on the circumstances. Discuss these potential responses with trusted members of your team and your community as you are developing them. Ask parents, for example, "If something bad happened here, and we responded to you in this way, would you feel confident in our response?" Review how other organizations and businesses have responded to crises and ask yourselves, "Is that how we want to be seen?"

Plan meetings with the complainant and/or his or her family. Meeting with a victim or a victim's family may not be an easy ask. They are likely to be angry and suspicious of your motives. But reaching out to them is part of your organizational mission to serve your community. Whether or not the accused committed the abuse alleged, these parents trusted you with your child. Reaching out to them provides you with an opportunity to express empathy for the situation and to reiterate your organization's duty to protect the children and youth in your program.

If you are successful in arranging a meeting with the victim's family, this is not a time to ask questions or investigate or debate whether the maltreatment actually happened. Rather, it is a time to meet privately and share with the family what you would share with any other family in your program—that you've received the allegations, that you are investigating, and that you will do what is necessary to bring healing, accountability, and closure.

Consider what resources you can offer to help bring closure. For example, if you have the budget, consider offering to pay for a certain number of counseling sessions. It's usually better to let the family choose a therapist, and you need to work with your attorney on how to phrase the offer without admitting liability. Don't let your attorney insist on a written release for any of these offers; now definitely is not the time to insert legalese into whatever relationship you can establish.

Address requirements of law enforcement and government agencies. In the scenario described above, it's more than likely that around the time you hear of your employee's arrest, you'll also receive a call—or maybe an unexpected visit—from law enforcement, child protective services, and/or licensing agency personnel. Be prepared to address these contacts.

First, any interaction with law enforcement should be handled by your attorney, if possible. In our practice, we often see law enforcement arrive at a client's office demanding immediate access to records and videos and to interview employees. While you don't want to appear defensive, it's also important to remind law enforcement agents that you have legal responsibilities to protect the privacy and confidentiality not only of the alleged victim but also of other children and youth in your program. Have your attorney gently remind law enforcement that, while you are happy to provide whatever they may require, you need a subpoena to protect your organization from any claims that you have released records in violation of state and federal confidentiality laws. Don't ever demand a warrant, as doing so may create the spectacle of seeing your facility raided on the evening news. But when you can do so without angering law enforcement, do explain the necessity of needing some legal document, such as a subpoena, before turning over records.

If possible, before delivering records and video to law enforcement or other agencies, make sure you have backups. Too often we have seen clients turn over records and videos without first making copies, thereby depriving themselves of the very evidence they need for an internal investigation.

INVESTIGATIONS

Once you've overcome the shock of the accusation and activated your IRT, you will need to fully investigate the allegations against your employee, volunteer, or other accused person. After your IRT has done its preliminary work, it needs to ensure you are investigating the incident or incidents thoroughly.

Internal or Independent Investigation?

When serious allegations of abuse, exploitation, or other serious harm have been made, there are two ways an organization can approach its response.

Internal Investigations. Some organizations faced with reviewing a child abuse claim prefer to conduct an internal investigation. If managed by attorneys, an internal investigation can help the organization keep the process and the results confidential. This is because, when attorneys are leading an internal investigation that is specifically designed to determine the underlying facts and provide legal advice, the attorney-client privilege applies to all aspects of the investigation. Such an internal investigation in a case involving child abuse or maltreatment can, as a result, be managed in a way that the organization is protected from disclosing the information obtained in the process, as well as the results, from disclosure to the public or to a claimant in a lawsuit. At the same time, to maintain that confidentiality, it is important that attorneys actually conduct and control the process. Simply having an attorney ask someone in the organization—the HR professional, for example—to conduct the investigation and report back may not suffice.

Internal investigations suffer from the problem that outsiders—the victim and family, the media, the community—may see them as simply an effort to "paper over" whatever occurred. As the old adage goes, "the cover-up is worse than the crime," and the public tends to view internal investigations in light of that phrase. In truth, internal investigations do sometimes display a bias towards protecting the organization. Because insiders are handling it, they often assume that the organization is right and may treat the claimants as opponents rather than potential victims. Internal investigations, therefore, are best for incidents or situations that are low-profile and not likely to garner public attention or call into question the organization's reputation.

Independent Investigations. Independent investigations are best whenever a problem is or likely to become public. What makes an investigation independent? While there are no specific definitions, there are a number of factors:

Are the investigators beholden to the client? Organizations seeking an independent investigation should consider retaining (1) investigators who have not done prior work for the organization and (2) who are obligated to independence and have no other duty to the organization.

Do the investigators have free reign? For an investigation to be truly independent, those charged with conducting it must have the freedom to interview whomever they desire regarding the matter; sufficient budget authority to carry out their work; and unrestricted access to any documents or other information held by the organization.

Do the investigators have independence to report? Often, the engagement agreement between an organization and its independent investigators makes clear that the organization may not modify the investigators' final report before it is released to the public. Contrary to popular belief, this requirement does not mean the organization cannot *view* the report prior to its public release, but it does mean that the investigators are free to accept or ignore any of the organization's proposed changes prior to the public release.

Trauma-Responsive Investigations

A critical issue for organizations to keep in mind is that those involved in a child abuse or similar investigation will be traumatized. A person who alleges he or she was abused is going through a traumatic event, whether or not the allegations are true. The accused has been shocked, either by the knowledge of his or her guilt or by the loss of faith experienced by those around him. Witnesses, co-workers, other employees, and organizational leaders are confronted with the realization that their conceptions of an individual may have been completely wrong. The individuals involved and even the organization itself, confronted with harm to a child in its care, an affront to its reputation, and a threat to its future, will react the same way a person might when facing any imminent threat: with a fight, flight, or freeze response.

Thus, when investigating a serious incident of abuse, the investigator needs to be sensitive to and aware of how this emotional reaction may affect those he or she is interviewing. For example, the "common sense" interpretation when a person avoids answering questions or seems anxious during an interview is to believe the person has something to hide. For a person who has suffered trauma, however, such a reaction is a natural effect of the "emotional" part of the brain overcoming the individual's ability to think clearly. When working in a crisis, an investigator must remember:

- Victims of abuse and those who witnessed such violations are often anxious and stressed.
- It takes time to build rapport, explaining why you are there, the purpose of the interview, and the steps you will take to care for them and, to the extent possible, protect their privacy.
- Witnesses want to know how their answers will be used.
- "I don't know" is an acceptable answer.
- To use open-ended questions, and never suggest an answer.
- To allow the person to tell the story in the order they wish.
- To use follow-up questions to clarify answers.
- Before leaving, explain what happens next.
- To ask if they need any social services, therapy, or other assistance for the trauma they have experienced.
- To avoid re-victimization. Don't interview them multiple times about a traumatic incident.

This list only scratches the surface of a trauma-sensitive investigation. There are many resources available if you wish to dig deeper into the effects of trauma on individuals responding to a crisis and how you might improve your ability to work with them. Be certain that whomever you entrust with your investigation knows all these important principles.

One important difference to note is that trauma-responsive investigation techniques *do not* require the investigator to believe the victim or search for the wrongdoer. Although some who advocate a trauma-informed response take this approach, it can be counterproductive. When an individual—child or adult—claims they have suffered abuse or are a victim, they may be telling the truth. At the same time, they may not. They may have suffered a *different* kind of trauma they are afraid to face, and making this allegation helps bring their pain to the surface. They may *believe* they are a victim of abuse without cause. Or they may have deeper issues that merit further exploration. In any of these situations, the investigator can remain objective while treating everyone with respect and empathy. Even the false accuser likely merits our compassion and understanding.

Responding well to a crisis starts well before the crisis hits. The more planning and tabletop exercises you can do in advance, the better your team will manage an actual crisis. Adapting these principles to your program will help you meet your obligations to your stakeholders and minimize the harm to your organization.

WORKSHEET #14

RECEIVING AND RESPONDING TO REPORTS: A TRIAGE PROCEDURE

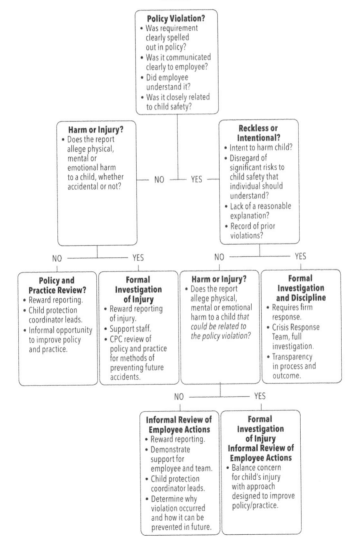

REPORT

Policy Violation?
- Was requirement clearly spelled out in policy?
- Was it communicated clearly to employee?
- Did employee understand it?
- Was it closely related to child safety?

Harm or Injury?
- Does the report allege physical, mental or emotional harm to a child, whether accidental or not?

— NO ┴ YES —

Reckless or Intentional?
- Intent to harm child?
- Disregard of significant risks to child safety that individual should understand?
- Lack of a reasonable explanation?
- Record of prior violations?

NO ———— YES

Policy and Practice Review?
- Reward reporting.
- Child protection coordinator leads.
- Informal opportunity to improve policy and practice.

Formal Investigation of Injury
- Reward reporting of injury.
- Support staff.
- CPC review of policy and practice for methods of preventing future accidents.

NO ———— YES

Harm or Injury?
- Does the report allege physical, mental or emotional harm to a child *that could be related to the policy violation?*

Formal Investigation and Discipline
- Requires firm response.
- Crisis Response Team, full investigation.
- Transparency in process and outcome.

NO ———— YES

Informal Review of Employee Actions
- Reward reporting.
- Demonstrate support for employee and team.
- Child protection coordinator leads.
- Determine why violation occurred and how it can be prevented in future.

Formal Investigation of Injury Informal Review of Employee Actions
- Balance concern for child's injury with approach designed to improve policy/practice.

WORKSHEET #15

Mandated Reporter Decision Tree

As with all of these worksheets, adapt this decision tree to reflect the laws of your jurisdiction.

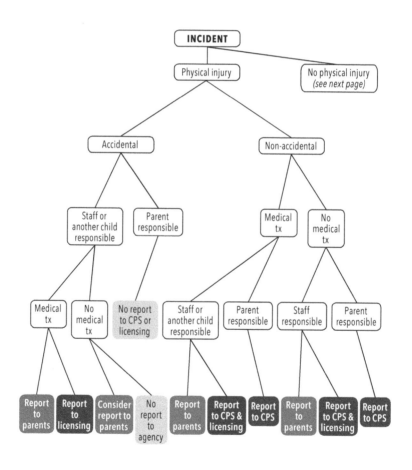

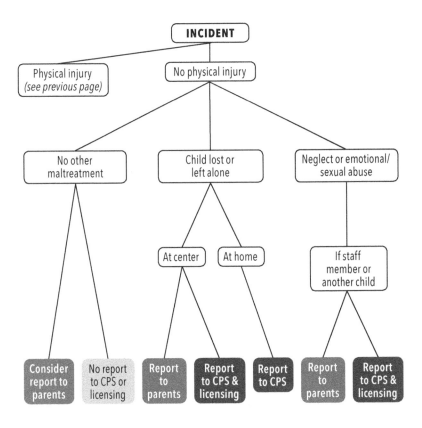

WORKSHEET #16

Responding to Incidents

Before the Crisis
1. Research and plan procedure for mandated report
2. Research historic insurance policies
3. Draft document retention policies
4. Draft communications policies and templates for statements
First 24 Hours
1. Suspend/isolate alleged perpetrator
2. Activate Incident Response Team
3. Make mandated report, if applicable
4. Notify insurer(s)
5. Draft public statement, if needed
6. Draft statement to parents of all youth in program, if needed
7. Obtain written statements
8. Gather relevant documents
9. Reach out to victim and alleged perpetrator
10. Plan meetings with employees and parents of youth in program, if needed
11. Respond to questions and requests from law enforcement and child protection investigators
First Week
1. Meet with parents of youth in program, if necessary
2. Follow-up emails with parents as needed
3. Report to Board and management
4. Start internal or independent investigation

Ongoing
1. Communicate with parents
2. Communicate with employees
3. Communicate with law enforcement, protective services
4. Work with insurance agent and/or assigned defense attorney
5. Complete internal or independent investigation

CONCLUSION: WRAPPING IT ALL UP

THIS BOOK HAD its genesis in our recognition over the years that too many of those failures we saw as professionals responding to child protection failures resulted from the same sort of dynamics as those that created Providence Canyon. Many YSOs make three basic errors in organizational thinking: (1) considering child protection as the task of one person, department, or section of the organization; (2) viewing incidents of child maltreatment as rare and stemming from the malicious intent of rare individuals rather than as a common danger that all YSOs must plan for; and (3) overreacting to human errors rather than figuring out ways to help prevent those errors.

In this book, we've tried to show you that protecting the children and youth you serve is not just a matter of creating personnel policies and tasking their enforcement to your HR department. Rather, those policies are an integral part of your organization's culture. Selecting the child protection policies you will implement requires making tradeoffs: how much risk are you willing to take, and will taking that risk enhance the joy that your staff and the children you serve experience? How can you vet employees and volunteers without discouraging or "running off" potentially good employees who have the best interests of youth at heart? How can you best protect the children and youth you serve while staying within a limited budget? We hope that this book has helped you to develop answers to those questions in a way that best suits your organization's needs.

We also hope this book has opened your eyes to the fact that protecting youth requires organizations to build not only a culture of protection but also a culture that values innovation and transparency and rewards curiosity and feedback. You should take from these materials a few lessons. Just because a lawyer recommends a policy doesn't mean it works for your organization. Just because others have implemented a particular policy doesn't necessarily make it right for your team. Many hands not only make light work; they also help build the kind of organization that not only keeps children safe but also succeeds in becoming a great place to work and a fun and safe place for young people.

After you've finished this book and have developed and begun practicing how you will implement your child protection policy, what's next? You might consider taking the approach of a book club in California that, after more than 20 years, finally finished reading and discussing James Joyce's novel *Finnegan's Wake*. What did they do after parsing this notoriously difficult read for over two decades? They started reading it again. Likewise, we hope that you'll continue to develop your child protection policies, reviewing them regularly, keeping them fresh, and adopting new ideas. And let us know what you come up with—we're always glad to help and learn.

ABOUT THE AUTHORS

Tom Rawlings is an attorney board-certified in child welfare and juvenile justice law. He has served as a juvenile court judge, as the child protection ombudsman for the State of Georgia, as the Director of the Georgia Division of Family and Children Services, and as leader of a child abuse prosecution and treatment team in Guatemala. Tom currently practices at Taylor English Duma in Atlanta, where he advises and defends youth-serving organizations. An honors graduate of Duke University and the University of Georgia School of Law, Tom earned a Masters' degree in International Human Rights Law from Oxford University (UK), and is certified by the National Association of Counsel for Children as a Child Welfare Law Specialist. He writes about child welfare issues at TomRawlings.substack.com.

Debbie Ausburn says, "I make my living as a lawyer, but what I *do* is take care of other people's children." For more than 40 years, Debbie has been working with at-risk children, starting when she was a preteen helping her parents with their summer camp and church ministries. In the years since, she has served as a juvenile court probation officer/social worker, group home parent, criminal prosecutor, volunteer, Board member, and attorney defending youth-serving organizations.

While still single and early in her legal career, she served as a volunteer foster parent for emergency placements. In North Carolina, she worked as a federal prosecutor of child abuse and violent crimes, and served as a foster-parent for respite care and long-term placements of abused children and teenagers. She returned home to Georgia, switched to civil law, and married a man with five children, two of them still at home. Most recently, she and her husband found themselves parenting the teenage child of a family friend.

In her legal practice, Debbie defends youth-serving organizations in cases ranging from accidents to claims of sexual abuse and advises them about best practices for protecting the children in their care. She is a sought-after speaker on topics such as mandated reporting of abuse, internal investigations, and developing youth protection policies. She blogs about legal topics at Insights.taylorenglish.com, and about parenting issues at OtherPeoplesChildren.org. Her first book, *Raising Other People's Children*, draws on her decades of experience with the foster care system to offer insight and guidance to foster parents, step parents and caregivers.